SELECTED POEMS

ALISON BRACKENBURY

Selected Poems

CARCANET

First published in 1991 by
Carcanet Press Limited
208-212 Corn Exchange Buildings
Manchester M4 3BQ

British Library Cataloguing in Publication Data
Brackenbury, Alison
 Selected poems.
 I. Title
 823.914

 ISBN 0-85635-924-6

 The publisher acknowledges financial
assistance from the Arts Council of Great Britain

Set in 10pt Palatino by Bryan Williamson, Darwen
Printed and bound in England by SRP Ltd, Exeter

Contents

Dreams of Power

My Old

My old are gone; or quietly remain
thinking me a cousin from West Ham,
or kiss me, shyly, in my mother's name.
(My parents seem to dwindle too; forget
Neat ending to a sentence they began,
Beginning of a journey; if not yet.)

Cards from village shops they sent to me
With postal orders they could not afford.
They pushed in roots of flowers, carelessly,
And yet they grew; they said a message came
To say the Queen was dead, that bells were heard.
My old are gone into the wastes of dream.

The snow froze hard, tramped down. Old footprints pit
Its smoothness, blackened footprints that I tread
That save me falling, though they do not fit
Exactly, stretching out beyond my sight.
My old are gone from name. They flare instead
Candles: that I do not have to light.

Derby Day: an Exhibition

The great Stubbs' picture of the great Eclipse
Hangs in the corner it defies,
Effortless. The great are luminous.
Orbed flanks shine solid, amber, having won.
A gold-red horse called Hermit won, and broke
The wild Earl of Hastings, who had flung
Woods and fields against. How can Eclipse
Comfort those eclipsed, who never won?

The young Fred Archer with a boy's sad face,
Shot himself, sick dizzy on the edge.
He won six flaring Derbys. Not that one
In which a woman sprang beneath the rail.
In thudding dark, pain tore all colours; died.

And yet a brilliant day. Do not mistake:
That which we do best kills us. Horse and man
Amber in the mist of downs, sea-shore,
The spring of wave, glow greatly. They survive

The Divers' Death

The two dead divers hauled up in their bell
died not from lack of air, but the great cold:
the linking cable severed and they fell
fathoms of dark, away from tides that rolled,
from gulls that rode the storm, from sun that warmed
down where the wind dropped; and the hands that cried,
used to much, not this. No breath
deserved the line to break, the spasm, black to death.

And so the dead child, taken quickly out
from white walls, the emptied woman. Or
brain-damaged babies, who can roll about
like small sea-creatures on the padded floor.
Someone washes them and listens for
their cries; they turned their heads when we went near.
But someone might have wished for them a knife
to exorcise the darkness of that life.

Deeper than the fast, bright fishes go
are the great depths that divers cannot kill –
what knife could cut so bitterly? And so
We are love's strange seabirds. We dive there, still.

These are the Colours

These are the colours. New, cold blue
which glints between the drifting packs,
the wasted dark of the long day,

pure snow, which fills and freezes in our tracks.

This is the region where the ships are caught
where gold-billed swans die heaving in the ice
to which the lode-stone sings with human voice

this song I sail into your northern eyes.

'Yesterday Vivaldi visited me; and sold me some very expensive concertos'

He had only one tune.
And that
a thin finger on pulses:
of spring and the frost,

                        the quick turn of girls' eyes

a tune

to hold against darkness,
to fret
for trumpet, for lute
for flutes; violins
to silver the shabbiness
of many towns
the fool's bowl, the court coat,
a tune he would give:
without sorrow or freedom
again, again

              there is only one tune.

Sell it dearly to live.

Riders

The days are spring, the nights are winter still,
The young mad girl (her morning hair
unkempt, wide violet smudges round her eyes)
tells of last night's fog, before the doors
are opened. 'In the end we walked two miles
pushing the bike. We'd follow the road's curve
till we lost that – When the white line was there
we'd follow that, until we lost our nerve –
    and cold! the frost was falling out the air.'

In cold, your child fell. Now when I ring
we talk a while till you must break away,
there rises out of dark his mastered crying
by which I'm torn. But what is good for you
is not for me: that cry distracts and chills.
    I have become a rider, on the hills,

piercing to slow grey counties under mist,
their crouching churches and their factories' glint.
While past all these your far hills rise
rough in their trees, shut from the sun; a hint
of dream, of meaning, as the horses fret
hot strength we barely hold – a tree-stump missed –
heads toss like waves' heads, pulled at bay; and yet
    I fell off jumping once and limp for this.

It's pain we ride: you with the black machine
you in the sweating ward, I tossing down
the great grey shoulder to the bruising earth.
And no kind bud but some strange seed from birth
grows separate from us; children do not save
love only just. Flesh shudders and flesh spills
and spent for whom? My cold vision aches:
    staring down for you from the high hills.

Fog frightened you because you could not see,
thick pain-drugs made you sick, I am afraid
almost brushing trees; speed's ruthless there,
saying yes then trying to control
quick consequence of all we chose to do.
Trim and wretched streets beneath my sight
a deep, far risk I praise and yours and mine
to raise and check the pain; to shiver, bear

when the paint is chipped, when spring's sharp night
Draws down white frost from overriding air.

Gallop

An unholy conspiracy
of girls and horses, I admit,
as never being part in it
but riding late and anxiously.
On Sunday when the horses climb the hill
scrambling the dried watercourse to reach
the open field to gallop: all my breath
swells hot inside me as the horses bunch
and pull for mad speed, even my old horse –

'Gently!' the leader calls – but they are gone,
hunters, young horses, surging hard ahead,
I rocked across the saddle, the wet soil
flung shining past me, and the raking feet
shaking me from stirrups as I speak
breathless, kind names to the tossing neck
haul back the reins, watching the widening gap
between my foundered horse and the fast pack,

wondering if I can keep on, why I do this;
and as he falters, my legs tired as his,
I faintly understand this rage for speed:
careless and hard, what do they see ahead,
galloping down spring's white light, but a gate
a neat house, a small lawn, a cage of sunlight?

And pounding, slow, behind, I wish that I
rode surely as they do but wish I could
tell them what I see in sudden space –
two flashing magpies rising from the trees
two birds: good omen; how the massive cloud
gleams and shadows over as they wait,
the horses blown and steaming at shut gates:
disclosing, past their bright heads, my dark wood.

The Wood at Semmering

This is a dismal wood. We missed our train,
Leaning on a bench, and happy while
The express, green, like a Personenzug
Slid past us as we sat there with a smile.
Tree draughts blow smells of earth to us and tug
A memory: a sadness, found again.

For in this place the nervous women meet
Summer, summer; watch their fingers shake
To splash a tonic water round the glass.
Where the widow, thin, brown-haired, will take
Her daily walk between the pines; will pass
Small cones and drifting flowers, with numb feet.

Past pale yellow foxgloves, small to ours,
Where harebells darken purple, she steps slow.
The toad-flax opens deeper mouths of gold,
The tiny eye-bright, high white daisies blow.
Rose of chill lips, small cyclamen unfold,
And touch her feet.

For earth has many flowers.

Night Watch

The cat curls in her fur, like a robe,
which is tortoiseshell, bright
black and amber
her paws glow white, she is
the most beautiful cat I have half-owned:
her name is 'Moth': she catches them,
and once, when young, moved lightly.

And I? I am hope, I am fear. In the long grass, we will
watch evening.
People are washing their children
eating their food.
It is very still.

When all floors were washed today
(Moth was lost, in sun) I lay
on the bed by the propped window:
by a blue-lit space
where swallows crossed and sank, and rose –
not to own the air but be
so free of it, to turn and fall
through pathless, sun-held sky
instinctive, ending, come so near,
on light wind wings softly tear
and close: flash sun: will never fly
through the open window

The sky is quickened: warm with light
always there, withdrawn from sight
to heat.
The clouds bloom slow:
from some distant rubbish ground
the gulls fly in straight lines, nicked wings
dark to tender light
calling harsh and slow, the sea
as distant here, as sky from me,
closed in their freedom, journeying.
Dew rustles through the hidden depths of air:
still, as long grass grows, the earth is moving.
The cat is night, black fur.
I wear the evening

Live

The cowboys fade: to London. The neat letters
dance upon the white steps, spell out LIVE.
What do they say? A house held under siege;
inside, men armed and silent. We can see
nothing happen, till two stretcher-bearers
duck into a cave of shadowed stairs.
'They raise the victim carefully'
trot beyond parked cars with weighted steps.
But they have let one arm fall free, drop down,
ruffling the blanket, with a yellow sleeve.

The dead do not have careful arms; have only
something without feeling hanging down
below a blanket, carelessly,
limper than the breathing body. Since
we cannot glimpse the colour of the hand
almost brushing pavements, since next day
(freed from the deep coldness of this breath)
we will know news and names and who he was
(a name we will forget, cannot pronounce)

since the dead have nothing; since the sleeve
is all we see, agree now, it is yellow;
not what the explosion raised, mad gold
roaring, flowing through the white façade;
say it is yellow, duller than the sun
rearing downwards over trembling roofs;
careless as the dead are, not yet cold.

The Two

do not fear
the golden wings

sun lit their tips
before they fell

all lips meet the shadowed sea
love pity no such ends.

your pity fits the careful man
who joined soft wax with feathers well

who fell alone: on a grey shore:
   on whom all love depends.

Intimates

You lived too near the ghosts. For they were kind
dry, warm as snakes you never feared.
Speak now of love to men whose eyes
are moist and cold,
unkind as the true world.

For you are woken now by evening's rain
(a snake would shiver, slip into the dark)
are startled as it smashes on hot land.
The sky-light leaks. Rain pricks against your wrist –
strange fingers slip the gold ring from your hand.

Two Gardeners

Too far: I cannot reach them: only gardens.
And stories of the roughness of their lives.
The first, an archaeologist, had lost
Her husband to the Great War; never married
Again, but shared her fierce father's house;
Lit oil lamps and humped bright jugs of water
Until he died. We went there selling flags
Stopped at the drive's turn: silenced by her garden.

White water-lilies smoked across her pools.
The trees were hung with musk-roses
Pale as Himalayas; in darker space
Gleamed plants as tall as children, crowned with yellow,
Their name I never learnt. Her friends had found,
Smuggled her seeds, and lush stalks, from abroad;
While she walked with her father's snapping dog
Or drew the Saxon fields of Lincolnshire.

The other lived in the cold Northern side
Of a farmhouse, split for the farm's workers,
(Where we lived then). Once she had been a maid,
Had two children for love before she married
A quiet man. Away from her dark kitchen
She built a bank, her husband carried soil.
There she grew monkey flowers, red and yellow,
Brilliant as parrots, but more richly soft.
She said I could help plant them but I dared
Not touch the trembling petals – would not now.
I have sown some; I do not look to see
Such generous gold and scarlet, on dark air.

Both live; I call them gardeners. And I grow
Angry for them, that they might be called
Typically English. They were no more that
Than sun or wind, were wild and of no place.
The roots of light plants touched them for a while
But could not hold them: when they moved
They left all plants to strangers

                 in whose dust
The suburbs' wind sucks up white petals round me
To look and see them in their earth-dark shoes
Skirts stained by water, longer yet than ours.

Dazzled by dry streets I touch their hands,
Parted by the sunlight, no man's flowers.

Summer in the Country

'Strawberries', 'raspberries', whisper the letters.
Until July is a taste, to hide
In reddened mouths, in fields which feet
Can't flatten, tall, soft throbbed with heat.
Where horses shaking gnats aside
Come slow to hand through the darkening grass

Where seeds fall too, from willow trees
(Rooted in damp, an ancient drain)
White silk clings to my back. I see
Small clouds pass slowly overhead.
Ask me nothing. In harvest fields
Drivers wear masks – cough dust; hear grain
Hiss credit; loss. But in the shade
Pale seed drops lightly over me.

The harvest ends. White webs of cold
Are strung across the sun;
The wind blows now no hint of fruit
But draught, unease, what's done; undone.

The House

It was the house of childhood, the house of the dark wood
four-square and safe, it was the second house
at least, to bear its name. The first was burnt: was charred
foundations, hidden by a timber yard.

I knew this in my dream: the house was same
and solid. All its yews, church trees, were strong
red wood of generations. As we came
out in the dusk sight heaved, house, orchard, gone.
Cold in the trembling grass we shivered there.
On open hillside, to the first stars' stare

I watched dark, unsurprised. I could remember
the bombers roaring low above the trees
to reach their high 'drome, though the war was done.
The house had strained and crumbled.
                                        There is only
                the old magic, forced out in new ways.
Hard through the dream's cold spring I raised
My house again. My bones and my heart ache
In every joist. The altered rooms are filled
With lovely light: the only house
Which kills in falling, which you must rebuild –

                In new wood boxes, apples there
All winter breathe out sweetness, in cold air.

Robert Brackenbury

Ancestors are not in our blood, but our heads:
we make history.
Therefore I claim
you, from dark folds of Lincolnshire
who share my name
and died two hundred years ago
you, man, remembered there
for doing good: lost, strange and sharp you rise
like smoke: because it was your will
all letters, papers, perish when you died.

Who burnt them? Wife or daughter, yawning maid
poked down the struggling blackness in the grate
or walked slow, to the place where leaves were burnt,
the white air, winter's. Slips of ash
trembled on the great blue cabbage leaves:
O frozen sea.

Why Robert, did
you hate the cant of epitaph so much?
leave action to be nothing but itself:
the child who walked straight-legged, the man,
whose house no longer smoked with rain, and yet
(soft scent of grass in other men's archives)
your name, to linger; did you trust
that when all shelves, all studies fell to ash
your kindness still might haunt our wilderness
a hand that plucks at us, a stubborn leaf
twitching before rain

                    or did despair
turn: whisper there how you were young
to burn and change your world: not enough done,
from that you turned
to silence and a shadowed wall; unkind
to family, to wife, and to that maid:

Who buried you, for love, in Christian ground.

I think that you had ceased to trust in knowledge.
You did not want the detail of your life
wrapped round us like a swaddling cloth; passed, known,
to shadow over us like a great tree.
The crumbling, merging soil, the high rooks
cawing out the black spring are for you;
now we must speak and act: make day alone.

In one thing I'll be resolute as you.
In white day in the thawing grass I'll burn
one letter, then the bundles; stare
at the cracked silvering of walnut bark:
and see what, in that grace? Not you,
your eyes of frozen dark.
Perhaps the combed light of the counterpane,
the hot breath, that is action, the mist closing

huddled in cloth:

        turned eyes, the smoke's sharp glow:

snatch back the half-charred letter. In the icy
blue, wasted leaves watch silent the unmaking
flames crumble white

too like a God forsaking
the heart to ash.

And though I made you, though
I should ask nothing of you,
I will turn against you, bitter
as the girl's mouth in the garden
tasting winter, ashes: glow
of fire that cannot warm us
or ever quite betray,
smoke that twists the cold hand
       in shapes I do not know.

An Orange of Cloves

Clove-scent: the dark room where the lovers lie
A closet smelling both of must and musk,
Which makes the head faint: rawer and more old
Than pale-flowered stocks which scent the dusk.

Caverns of dark I entered first: I thought
I have danced here, and to a golden lute.
Branched velvet, rushes, gallows in the sunlight –

Sense shudders till it glimpses in a space
The great sharp-scented tree, its flowers, its fruit
All of a season, beating in the rain;
The orange, cloves cross-cleft; and past the pain,
A dark tree fading, seeding in each face.

Four Poems

I

Strange sea: sudden sea: no thing can be the same.
I think of snowdrops and lit hedgerows which
may never have been there.
What lay in that drink that we should stare,
the birds shout salt and harsh; black ways
gape between the water and your eyes?
I burn and my bones melt to gold.
And as I grip your hard wrist and we rise
I understand how our love lies:

not in waves' green light but light's great cold

II

By the king's trees I walked afraid.
You spoke your riddles tenderly:

Is not the moon's cold rising made
To lure the salt sea from the land?

Is not the horse which bolts with you
Gentle in stall, to brush your hand

And the amazing cherry tree
Rooted in possibility?

Silence. The dazzling boughs above
Dance white belief I dare not prove.

III

I am the maid who slept with you
To cheat you on your wedding night.
Mine is the mouth that parts on you
questing, till the birds cry light.
You the dark shape on the cliff,
my dreaded lord, my lovely man,
No maid or woman in the world
can hate or take you as I can.
My feet crush thyme. The fluid lark
Fuses your voices, Tristan, Mark.

IV

It could go on for ever so; the giving
As the sea melts into the autumn haze
I could wear out my weariness with love
Not knowing yet which shadow cools my days
Black king; a young man on a sunlit deck.
Fearing the wrecks where seas in winter break
I walk the garden's walks alone and plant
Two autumn crocuses the tall winds shake
To shivered blue of eyes. You wrote to me
We might at least 'preserve intensity'.
Not quite Isolde; but the crocus lit
To stranger flame. Through fear and work's ache we
Read the dark's story; risk; since one forgot
To change the heavy sails from black to white
Another died. As in an older story
The grieved man leapt from cliffs, crashed down in light.
The lark lifts struggling but she frees her voice.
Our business is avoiding tragedy.
My double flower: give me no choice
Between black ships and empty sea.

Dreams of Power

Note

Arbella Stuart (1575-1615) was the orphaned
granddaughter of Elizabeth of Hardwick, keeper
of Arbella's aunt, the dethroned Mary Stuart. She
was briefly married to William Seymour, great-nephew
of Lady Jane Grey, and died in the Tower of London.

Five winter days were lit by the slow thaw:
a light space in the window's frost shows us
my grandmothers: King Henry's threadbare niece;
Elizabeth in richest black, who crossed
from merchant's bed to Earl's: unloving looks
must have snicked between them, as they walked
the gold-edged carpets in the smoking light.
Margaret's son lay coughing in his bed
with the shy girl, my mother, sent 'to nurse'
thrust in the scented room and the doors closed.

The cold of those five days is in my heart:
old eyes appraising and the whispering.
My bed's long curtains with their yellow flowers
hiss serpent's breath, soft perfuming
which they laid round the young Elizabeth
to sweeten her pale boy. He married her;
dolls have no power
                          although a dark eye saw,
crumpled him in a strong room in the Tower.
Some jewel or promise, in my mother's dress,
undermined his warder for an hour.
And so my life burst in: between damp walls
with awkward coupling on a narrow bed.
I leave with her; duck, from the guard's eyes
down rocking stairs, go down the roofless yard
in a dark softness which the late rain frees
which I know, and the shuddered open body
(down which, the thick cloak pulls)
rises to moon's glitter, floating high.
Above the battlements the young moon swells,
she heaps great tides and yet would not destroy,
shut out day from this high glass or keep
virgin, the white fruit of winter's sky.

*

My mother was the true moon, quietly
she sank through dark. Words do not hold their love;
they give back sudden, sharp to me
a scent I sometimes trust to be her own.
I am 'Arbelle' to Mary's quick French voice;
Grandmother's 'Arbell!' as a hound is called.
I am Arbella. If you think this voice
should beg or teach, forgive me – ghost:
look through our names. The glass is black,
the boy is dream's dark air; whose coldness blows
through me, finds me separate; strangely grown:
a prison filled with dogs and scratching monkeys,
red silk, and scraps of song, becomes my home.

Mary (of whom my grandmother held care),
my godmother, had married, till eyes hardened
that twisted boy my father's brother. Air
exploding gold, he fled the shaking house –
garrotted by her lover in a garden.

Mary drew blood. I watched her flare to power
tease with the old Earl, with tender eyes;
spit like a cat at her embroiderer's wife.
Then her chins were double, her hair dyed:
her voice was silk. She wound me in for life
poor trembling fish! Pity and charm, pale sun's light
crossing the clawed bedcover, she drew gently
inside her circle, worked: In my beginning
is my end. 'I do not understand,'
the young men flushed – she laughed. Did she?

Wisdom to her was emblems. She was Papist;
which even then, I feared. I loved cold light.
Canvases framing hearts and appletrees
diverted her, she claimed; impulsive, bright
she was a child, never fearing time
(her will bequeathed to me her Book of Hours)
but she feared pain, and new pain clawed her heart.
From her safe bed she gave me dusty sweets,

I coughed on sugared roses, as she told
how she had slept in Scotland on the moors,
wrapped in a plaid; woke there, the horses still
like stone; the live breath smoking; the great hills
melting in light, as in her chaplain's hand
the small, protecting cup shone ringed with gold.
I told my grandmother, half-doubting this.
She stared. 'She made some play to hold her rule
and much too late. She told me she had sewed
in Council; never listened –' There she stopped;
the room's vast dark her judgement: fool and fool.

Loud and short the final quarrel came:
Mary with her dogs and scrambled silk
banished. She did not say goodbye to me:
she died then; when they sent the gilded book
years on, it hurt me, thinking her alive.
The circle ended. I could not begin.
In her scrubbed room I sniffed the dustless air,
the day was white with Derbyshire's cold spring.

'God be my judge, they dare not send her back!'
Now those eyes find my sleep. Then at our prayers
they read each text of vengeance until Hell
where Mary was, rose in their blaze of black.

*

They scolded my sharp tongue. I knew it came
from her; I would to God that it could cut
her picture from her frame, turn night to day
show you the kind of marvel that she was,
as beautiful as the great birds of prey
that ruffled in her mews. Where Mary sagged,
her skin grew taut, a white light lit her bones;
and so at forty-eight she caught her Earl,
she killed him too. She split each family
she married into, clawed them with contempt.
I will not list her marriages and beds,
her inventories do that. But I declare
all legends of her true, even her dying
(although I was not there).
Some fortune-teller told her she would live
until she ceased to build. She'd credit that,
though strong she looked for strength; burnt my hair-clippings
lest witches took them; had some private crafts
I know but cannot prove. The mortar froze.
The Chatsworth builders shrugged and turned for home.
She drove there in her carriage, raged at them,
for her cold eyes they heated cauldrons – nothing
could warm the frost. She saw the wall abandoned,
dragged home, and in the valued, dark bed died.
She was like the cold winds where she grew
her hating left mine feeble when it flared;
her stone initials raised to sky the only
emblem or human sign for which she cared.

II *Interregnum*

I am no emblem: and my name
is light
as pale silk or thistledown
too bright
for those who hold the signet and the seal.
Men weary of the old capricious Queen,
I come too late: their eyes look for a boy:
I make stiff-skirted curtsey to the Queen.
Her gold eyes flicker through me –
this royal glove, this toy –
for whom some perfumed closet is the place.

By boat we leave the slippery stairs. How far
the Queen's Thames swells in bursting tides of power,
too rough to hold my young and frightened face.

*

Our flowers were not as yours. You would not understand
how bluebells and small primroses shone warm
in our great gardens; they were all we had.
The flowers were gone with spring. Oh there were roses
pouring down each arbour and incline –
the damask and the musk
the briar and eglantine –
drenching us with sweetness till July
when they dropped brown and brittle. Freeze the spring:
our wisdom knew no second flowering.

*

Come dance with me, on gallery and stair,
my dance of idleness.
The dark spy codes: 'A lady shut in chambers
the English will not take into their hearts.'
I learn to sing (though with too thin a voice),
to sew with subtle thread,
to ride when storm and pestilence
allow me from the house: I learn the arts
of the noblewoman, or the small white dancing bear.

Also I learn Hebrew and speak Greek
and read the Bible daily without love.
I have one friend: my chamber's maid Jane Bradshaw
who combs my pale hair. At twenty-eight, lean moons,
the prisoned years close round me. You who are
stunted and chill, I stumble in your dance.
How painfully we lean to touch, how far
the great Thames swells – but that is not my tune.

It is time to think upon New Year
to make the Queen a present for this time.
Derbyshire under rain pours blue and green
along the window in the gallery –
yes, light enough, Grandmother. I can see.
It is the high time of her final house;
back we were carried, back where she was born;
in her new palace on a bitter ridge
like birds we huddle, shaken by the storm,
no Queen's at Hardwick; now she does not care
but measures the cream curving of her stairs
touches her tapestries. If dreams are grown
a prison, this is one, I hate each stone –
but in my hate, less power than Mary's had.

Here blow great hangings Mary never saw.
I tell her of them: 'Smouldered red brocade
has made a gown for tall Penelope.
She is not me. Although my eyes flash dark
she stares like Grandmother. Sometimes I see
your chestnut wildness in her. Gentle God
whose stern books I read coldly, let me free
out of these ghosts of power. This here is me:
Perseverance (worse worked); she is holding
a pale ungainly bird, that flaps to fly.'

In my hands flutters the uncrumpled lawn:
the Queen's white veil. Slow fingers, it is time
to edge, with silver thread that hurts the hands
honeysuckle, trailing like a star
along the border; I draw tiny things
most curiously and well and without love.

I cannot walk into the villages – the pox is there;
hate me: I do not care

my gentleness is folded in myself.

I have become the mistress of my dreams.
Grandmother watches less; I stay in bed
ignoring the dark morning; though it tugs
in my bed curtain and its yellow flowers.
Caterpillars curl along the frieze
they shiver, gold. I close my eyes again.
Arbell, says the far voice, it is time –
I am Arbella and I walk with him
through a sea-city, light rings like a bell.
The morning is my kingdom. I am walking
among the children in a high salt air
(warmer than London's streets) and my long skirt
is lit with silver and disturbs no dust.
But his hand? I cannot hold it. Fading
as the gold air. I cough. The late wind whines,
secrets fever me – hunched warm and close
above her veil, in the dark window seat,
reaching past a needle to a hand –
as though the cold air pricked me with its heat.

They bring in white candles to gentle the shadows.
My flourished veil is well-received. The Queen
sends a mean present but with kinder words
'would know how it is done'. I tell you, lady: keep
a soured nature in a winter house
as flowers drop silver, as the thin blood weeps.
So Mary's gifts were made. Sharp heart, laid to waste:
let this year spin me more than thread and sleep.

                              *

I had a cousin I had never seen:
I plucked grey quills, as snow falls, from the wing
of that ungainly bird my figure held –
                    and many were the letters that I wrote.
I shudder now to feel them locked and lying
in a dry chest, their blots and wildness bare
for any eyes. For like a spare bright glove,
I set my cousin's name on my starved hand,
I wrote his guardian, asking we should meet –

I do not now recall I mentioned love.

The weather, strangely mild. The black mare was not mine.
Was she made hounds-meat with that willing mouth
that quickening change of paces to my heel –
I would have buried her, for love. I must
call back that riding time: the hills a shimmer
in sheets of light, of silver and sharp black.
Dreams are as stuffs of dresses; you can feel
a quality where fingers brush. As wind
rushed my new life, I touched a roughness there:
too cold, too fixed. I struck the small warm flank,
along the hill's spine, galloped the black mare –
too fast, as the groom called. Words, horses, are
obedient, reckless; as those who ride.
Such sure feet did not fail. But all next day
the hills lay brown and sodden; almost silent
the Queen's men rode, sailors, on the mist's tide.

*

Do you still trust? Then never trust your kin:
my cousin sent my letter to his Queen.
I trust he had a fat purse for New Year.
To me, came Henry Brounker, a broad man
in brown-caked riding habit (foundering
through mud for days to check my misbehaving).
His greeting words creaked stiffly as a door.
Grandmother would have beat me if she could,
(her thin unloved granddaughter, turning wild),
assured him of her loyalty; she could,
being most loyal to herself. And I
left to the questioned air, cried like a child –
not at first, to them. But trust your kin.

I tested all the weapons of the weak;
I started with my mad self-pitying dream.
Imagined loves I twisted through my talk
and wrote at night strange, endless letters; streams
of words washed down my paper. Then as now
words were my country; then they failed me. How
can tears' heat see clear enough to write?
See true. It's hard. How sadly and how cold
I see my lit hair tangled in those nights
my blind hand scribbling, telling Brounker how

41

I loved the Earl of Essex – two years dead –
who had seemed to like me, as a child,
and when I spoke too loud, defended me.
(No wonder. He picked every losing cause:
a ready talent, which excuses me.)
At twenty-eight I should have looked beyond
those brilliant hazel eyes to policy.
But dead and lovely and my ally still
I summoned him: a ghost may write to ghosts,
as a slow girl retreats to thoughts of school.
But we forget too much: the murdering hosts
he could not check in Ireland; how he would
have rooted London up to snatch the Queen.
A word united us. The word was Fool.

I agree with good Erasmus: Folly
is a fine woman and she strips us bare.
Brounker spent hours noting answers, shaking
my branches, seeking treason's apples there.
'Who were your lovers?' he demanded 'Names –'
The long flames flashed: I said 'My cousin James.'

He dropped his pen. The slobbered Scottish King!
His mouth hung open as the black ink spread.
I hissed triumphant. I was Queen and Eve
but mocking blew love's candles from my head

and left me on a cold-lit, lonely stage.
I loathed each scene and like a drug drew more.
Sent up the right stair from the Gallery
I entered, flaring, through the left-hand door.
They started, cold: a second, I had been
the royal phoenix, heiress of her blood.
What did Grandmother say; to shatter me?
And why did I return? Some word, some note? I could
sustain no noble act. My memory
melts tricks and scenes like snow, and finds beneath
a fevered mind, the impotence of rage –
the Queen's fox-red so briefly flamed my hair.
I turned the mirror. I had left the stage.

Then, as far lust and intrigue fell away
I clawed against the windows to be free.
I would not eat while I was in that house:
that was the sharpest gift they gave to me:
that I could die. Mary had lingered, fat.
My face grew hollow and I seemed to see
faces behind their own. I pushed away
the tainted chicken and the sugared pap.
And so I gained my only victory.
They let me leave Grandmother, carried me
to Wingfield, the old house where I lived
spoilt by grooms and tutors, as a child.

And such I felt, lying in the great bed,
as weak as after birth. Then as I learned
the old Queen died on cushions without sound –
night courtiers spurred to Scotland – the spring tide
rushed up the Thames, till round my sleep, it turned.

IV   *The Court*

Dark pendulum,
swinging time,
are you invented yet?
The centuries blur lightly.
The sharpest eyes forget.
But Court clocks chime.
Allow me to present
a true and most un-Christian
Testament.

I leave my best brocade
(white roses at its hem)
to the girl who vomits, after feast,
while courtiers cry 'Amen'.

Next best, my chastity,
I leave the Maid of Honour with red hair
(so recently returned to Court); or to
the wailing child left in a tenant's care.

I leave my thin waist to the heavy Queen.
Also my pregnant mind, to swell
in her, who made us sit upon the floor
to play at childish games. Since she was kind,
(grin not so, Death), I also wish her well.

I leave beside the nervous King, a dream:
a great moth which by moonlight bangs the pane
a window with no ready catch
that he
may hold no wretched soul at court again
lying of his love to them. But pause,
he dreams already (Death says) of worse things.
The moth is drowned in blood. Strike out that clause.

I leave my soured mouth and aching head
and my great debts, to hell,
which would suit courtiers well,
but not my servants; give them better days.

Observe that I do not bequeath my heart.
What lover's hand was cut
by the sharp tongue of art?
To you, I give the petalled truth of names.
     So I the noble Lady the King claims
     'guid cousin' – and too fully in my mind,
     leave all – except the Court of my lord James.

*

And yet I laughed, when first at Court,
innocent, at a Christmas play.
(My lodgings lie against the street
smudged with November, muddied grey.)
Far shines the young and shuttered hand
my sly and red-haired Chaplain took,
who called me lovely, learned, said –
my frail sixteen-year body shook –
if he could serve me, I must speak.
And while I trembled, fallen, bright,
he was packed off, within a week.

Too near, my steward quietly
brings in black books for tallying.
'Sit down,' I say. But to my side
he stands, unadded; trembling
only when I turn suddenly,
caught by a blacker line: 'I see
the yellow pearls are pawned again.
You must redeem them next month for
the birthday masque.' (Young eyes fix dark,
Mine blur from focus.) Then the Queen's
plump birthday gift –

                they think me poor
whose jewels and dress – as he contrives –
might feast a cottager for life.
Everyone I know has debts
they never pay. (Have I paid Hugh?)
My fine nose quivers. He has spun
some threadbare plan: a short-term loan.

Relieved, I praise. His cheek rots red.
So, dreamer, I am set for sale:
And you would save me? Yes, it would
be a warm, an easy bed;
though ladies marry stewards, this
is mockery; a fairy-tale
of second-best, sad charity.

Carts rumble: a girl begs and calls
in high chill whining 'pity me,'

he shuts the thick door softly. That is all.
That earth could freeze...

                    The streets smell foul.

                    *

Cloud shadows drift the bank. On Hugh's old cloak
Jane and I count scratches; down hill paths
Hugh rode into the villages to seek
a carpenter. The coach leans where gorse burns;
stung gold, I see the axle snapped in half.
The groom's boy, whistling, trots each horse in turn
between the banks, through brown and dying may.
Such is my summer progress through these parts,
bumping the tracks, avoiding pedlars' carts;
stopping at will; but when our slow path crossed
Hardwick's glittered shadow. There breath paused.

The coach broke – first – soon after. I sent Jane
in a low shop where once they let me buy
ribbons for pearled dolls. Jane found a fine
red flannel – it would line our winter skirts,
the woman said, come out to me; her black
sharp eyes grew falsely tender as she cried
I had been gone too long – I should come back:
and Jane drop more true coin in her hand?

No, beggars are the debt we cannot lose:
warmed and sore, I watch a new group come,
their long coats patched with purple, like a bruise:
they set a child down and watch her keenly
clutch the wild, white roses they have sent,
constantly spilling petals in their spent
light glow: the white face of a gentle child.
Hers is hard brown. The clenched hand without
the roses needs a crutch. Slow as she comes
dispassionate sun lights on the hanging foot,
the long red scars. She halts, unsure

47

before the bank, the cloak; swings round to see.
They shout. Uncomprehending like a dog
she shivers, ducks and thrusts the flowers at me.

Do you dream I bought her, like a horse?
a child I could have touched but for a sense
she'd bite? Death clawed her where no words can soothe.
Uneasily I bend to her and ask
'Who hurt your foot?' Not words but smells of alms
open this rose. Her sharp teeth shine. She smiles
'Dog got me, lady, up at Marchand's farm.'

Hardwick had dogs. The dark eyes flash five years
when I slept here, in winter's flowered bed;
Jane stares in warning but I hand the child
what my purse holds. She turns, black pupils flared,
small, hopping dust, she leaves as light as bird!
they will keep my money; she is spared
a beating till tomorrow: all I bought
of one day's sun. In light streets where Hugh calls
the son comes, the old man sleeps by damp walls
through fevered June the white dust drifts and falls.

Jane's brown eyes wonder what to say to me.
Beggars are vermin, though the child was lame.
If I sold all my jewels and won the King
I could buy land. I could live here again.

Nor Queen nor wife, half-fumbling, I would spread
warm in a quiet kingdom – much misled,
my wilful self denying, some slight good.

Kind dream. Far sun. Do your eyes give it home?

You know your clouds. I must describe my own.

*

48

Autumn was warm. I wondered; often fled
from fumes of court and from the golden air,
I pleaded a sick head
slipped Whitehall before supper. Then I wrote
quick as the light caressed me, to a friend
late gone from Court: who left me a white dress
gold with honeysuckle, peaches – unworn, but too voluptuous
too young – too rich to waste.
                                         'If any land
should be set for sale in our cold country,
I beg that you will let me know at once.
Concluding, Madam, your most loving friend.'

I do not sleep. I will survive a while:
in which I can bear London, hear the river
lapping the long houses, undecayed,
till my new dream, my garden is half-laid.
I plant its twisted paths with camomile
with thyme and rosemary; sharp scents there rise
from feet; sharp chaffinch cries; in hedges, closely twined
strength marries sweetness, hawthorn clasps rose briars.
Arbours, I train; set tables, deep in leaf.

If money grows I will fetch rareties,
fritillaries: great ruby butterflies
to thrust the snow (beside what hedges hold:
violets, that lend sleep; cowslips; the hazed
blue of forget-me-nots. I must confess
though I was trained in still-rooms, I was lazy
to learn of plants. Now I will raise my own).
With gilliflowers, the late pinks, I will try
to coax the North's late summer past July.
Diligent at evening I will look
through neighbour's herbals, legendary books
which mingle strange and sweet, and lie about them all.

Marigolds blaze in every half-kept yard
outside my gate; I'll not forget – The garden
lingers, unmade, into my sleep and claims
a dark elusive scent: a flower no herbal names.

V *Meetings*

I hated fooling; round the windowseat
the bright heads gathered, teasing round his name;
though he was young from Cambridge, new to Court
what pricked me was my sharp dislike of them.

'Lady! sweet William will not speak with you,
he only reads.' My title's snow, sad power
to freeze. 'You gentlemen are ignorant:
such ignorance has named me too, a scholar.'

The face turned flushed. My glance lit on grey eyes;
then, as he bowed, indeed the student's bare
thin fingers. Something warmer crossed his face,
perhaps he did not see me but a dress:
spring's hem of white   gold throat of summer's fruit.
Still cold I watched the others drift from sight
dropped my name in a flattering drink of light
where black glass shone behind a draughty seat.

Mistrust such plays for power. Dangerous, distracting were

the dancers in far noise.
                              I kept aside
the stiff skirt darker gold. We spoke of much.
His slow voice touched against the poets' Greek,
to me cold voices, cry of migrant birds
music too late for truth. I turned this speech
quickly to mock, cry dreamer. If he heard
it did not reach; he asked, light eyes assured,

'Where shall our names live, lady; but in books?'

Not yours, I shook, not mine, the face
the glass held, trembling, bright,
into the dark where I felt frost gleam hard.
I rose. I saw his manners fall away:
the hand he reached to shrank like snow
sensing the Court's noise rising, tides of gold,
low, absurd I heard him say
I had saved him; I was his 'gracious moon':
that he would ride and thank me in bright day.

50

Alone, too quickly I let fall the dress.
There was an ink-stain half-scrubbed on the hand
I took too lightly. I must face him soon,
I who thought love dignified and kind, stand:
with ten years fading, scuff the dress –
gold dancer, bare feet tingling, sudden dark
dissolving every sense in foolishness,
mistrust the shows of power.
All that sustain me are
the roses on my skirt

Roses of air and fire

                     *

This is the letter I shall write to you,
between the candle's smoking and cold dew.

my dark dove and my dear
I fear you are too young
that for you light springs
in all you look upon.
Although I smile and tell you lies,
come close, there is old darkness in my eyes.

In spite I turn all mirrors to the wall
and watch myself swim small into your eyes,
lost in your depth of light you cannot know
there is a burning coldness makes me wise.
I beckon you, dressed in my borrowed flame
my masquing gown, you trot towards the snare,
I would cry to save you, you would leap –
but it is winter and the tracks are bare
and give no cover or escape but draw
slowly to my forest's dark
my dear

– who held his hand out to this fire. Lest
you see – conceit I give the coals. But bright
it fills the glasses' fingered emptiness
sharp, tender, blue: spring crocus tricked by light.

*

This fugitive and winter love
silvers the lips to frost. I wake, and shine;
the lean trees have no sap to write of us
– nor any rag of leaf, that we may hide.

Bare twigs beat at our faces as we walk.
Jane lingers after like a plump, dark, bird.
Wind pulls my hair loose from the golden pins,
and snatches all our speech, but for a word.

I dare not write. One frozen afternoon –
cold birds – we huddled on the draughty floor.
You kissed my throat in firelight. The logs flowered.
Jasmine, clear yellow for the winter sun
burned on the sills. In darkness, half unsure,
the wind's dogs scratch the thick transparent door.

*

Am I unkind? Before the Council, I
answered all, admitted nothing. They
might know with Brounker, I had cracked to glass,
but that was in a younger, fainter day.
Now on my unpaid gown and upright chair
the window's light was hardening. I sat cold.
When they informed me he had bought
their peace with tears; and a declaration
he would not treat of love with me again;
unshocked I told them 'I am sorry for it'
would not blur sight through tears, as women should.

Pity is not softness. Cold I wrote
reminding what he owed –
I knew that I could break him if he came.
I did not accuse but waited till
(shocked from out his books into my arms)
he cried, that he had given them his name.
I stroked the fine hair slowly; love: it's hard
to be strong to them who always come
too early, wake us shaking at a time
too unexpected, young;
when we are tender, and their cold eyes kind.

*

VI *Marriage*

2 a.m.

The good die now, this cold clasped to their heart.
If human faces watch, they do not see.
Into death's dark I marry; yes, in part
as she my dead grandmother would have done
to suit my horoscope. The blacker art:
by dawn the ruffling birds will whistle, see
Jane and Hugh; the slow priest in whose church
we planned this (may the old cruel God forgive).

Candles blow breaths of cold. The new ring burns
gilt on my tender skin. Still cruel? to live

touch Jane's chill cheek, and strangely, Hugh,
leaning miles, trailing light; to keep
your quick cold hand in mine. Your scared eyes glow:

the black wicks smoke, we part, too late for sleep.

*

Such grace, your clumsy fingers made:
your gentleness held even when we failed,
and laughed, for reason that the night has kept;
that fumbled, likely bed, let your eyes close;
your hand smoothed on my small breast, and you slept.

Half-choked beneath the tightness and the fear
yet body opens generous as flame.
I dream, circled in fire. I am here
light with nowhere. Light becomes your name.

By falling coals we scrambled for your clothes,
I pulled the white shirt over your slow head,
I rubbed my hands against you till you warmed.
You spoke me in a new voice sleep had thickened
and left me in the dawn, my vacant bed.

I walked between the beech trees' silver flesh.
Blunt ash buds stroked the sky. The Court and park
hung secret as the face your hands have framed.
The night you did not come, I slept; exposed
in dream, you hammered, building us an ark:

I said, 'He will not save us though he could'
(the constant knocking at the house door rose)
Where are you? So. Since no man drowns in tears
and since He does not kill and it is known
(my door is next) love's naked, wrecked in dark –

Dress quick. It is still cold. The high seas spurn
the wicked; leave them clothes and life alone.

                    *

That I knew you so briefly, now I grieve:
that I cannot remember, as I ought,
between cupped hands, a flame: that jerks sideways
and stings my wrist and yet remains
as luminous and tender as you were.

Do you still read? They have you in the Tower
whose cold invades the heart, as Raleigh knows
whose son has died for him in El Dorado.
I did not want your pain; not that hard power.

Yes, the good Bishop is my warder still.
I hope Hell has him. I admit I made
our journey out of London misery.
I screamed and took to bed. He was delayed,
ruffled from his wine, by such raw pain.
I did not have to act. Does dignity
still weigh with you? You are more dear to me.
Forgive. That's what he preached. Humility
obedience. How wicked, love, to grow
so wild, to weep. They carried me outdoors.
And now we are in Durham where the snow

is warmer than the wind – I never knew
such cold existed, till this northern world.
The town is small, the winds enormous. Hugh
brought a half-frozen bird down from the sill:
once fed it scrambled back into the storm.
(The people here speak lilting, strangely, Will,
their voices rise like birds.) Here you keep warm
and that is all. I will not see his Grace –
forgive; I am not sourer; I am warm
with Jane, and grow, to creatures, strangely kind.
I eat no meat. We live like creatures, here,
driven to draughty holes. Now I would like
some cat, some dog, to breathe upon my bed
but would not poison them. How Mary kept
monkeys; I told you that?

I will not say
I wished for months that I had borne your child
(though in a week from when they came, I knew)
and yet there is that vein of coldness in me –
the suckling done, would she have plagued me? Well
I keep no monkeys. And I will not say
still dazzled after sleep, I reach for you.

Your letters worry me. Have you been ill?
Can you see trees? Sunlight is hard here, clear
in ice-edged branches at the river's edge
held out of the flow. I feel you changed;
dreams should not freeze as I am frozen here.

I end in hope. His Grace leaves word: the King,
now I am quiet within my cage, may let me
like some unnatural bird, go South for spring.
I send you flowers, though they are Durham's snow,
furring the sill, upon the blue glass, thickening.

VII *Escape*

'Think,' I urge, 'when you were newly married,
if you had been kept from him for so long –'
her hand puts down the apple it has peeled.
She smiles at me, this soft and fair-haired woman:
lady of a house so lightly guarded.

I am glad your letters turn more tender –
or could I cheat her so? Let my eyes close:
I see my worn face bent to kiss your shoulder.
Through fire's kind heat, I shiver. (I have been ill.)
                                        'You know
it is arranged; but for one night alone.'

The apple peelings, delicate, flush brown.
Her warm face is left shining by my lies.
Look in the books, good dreamer, for her name
which I have forgotten. With no shame –
I honour still the kindness of those eyes.

I wear, for her, the full set of men's clothes:
soft boots, the muffling cloak, the swaggered sword.
She laughs until she chokes: a trick I use,
a glancing humour: as a mirror whirled
comes back with all the world behind your head.
She pours me wine. The ceiling flashes swords –
finished, I plant upon a chair, astride.
Passing me the glass, her fingers shake,
as do my own. For I am terrified.

*

In the wet yard, the lantern wavering,
they brought another horse. I only wished
a friendly ditch: to lie, until the ache
left me and the noise of horses died.
Raw brandy dazzles eyes. The groom's boy, opening
a yellow space of kind light blurred by straw,
turned the tired horse to watch them heave me on.
I heard him tell the groom across the door
'That gentleman will not hold out to London.'

Before you see the road or smell the fight,
That voice says 'you will not –' and fades to night.
I cannot hold this horse, unschooled and pulling strong.
I have not ridden all the prisoned year,
I never rode astride. My soft thighs run
into a childish quivering of pain –
as pot-holes drop, again, again I'm thrown
at the sharp pommel; or I snatch the mane.
The rattling riders call, but dare not use my name,
I do not speak; as if my silence would
drown out their rough feet on flint and mud,
their pace that aches my arms and numbs my blood.
I scarce see low Orion; the snatching trees; my hands
translucent from the sickness, burn with cold
in clumsy gloves, claw back the dangerous rein.

Out of the jolting dark, words beat my head
to drive back the boy's whisper in the yard,
not gentleman – hold out to London – will not –
cold heart, as tired legs stumble, I rise jarred,
my body, urgent in its pain, knows what
the worn hoofs beat: that harmony is hard.

*

Where the black river-waters hissed
they pulled me down, I looked for you:
strained through the dark, I would have kissed
your cold mouth there for ever, but they said
you were delayed; climb in the boat.

I drifted fevered, stupid love.
(The boatman stared at my white hand,
drawn fretful from a man's hot glove.)
Dimmed moon in fog, our ship's light dipped.
(Come late, you found another ship.)
The fog had filled our minds. All captains plead
the turn of tide: too weakly, I agreed.

Slowly, we entered on the open sea.
Enormous waste. I leaned against the rail
in a dark, strange gown Hugh had for me.
I rode the tilting till my sickness died.
I spoke to no one. All I heard
was sea; or from the rigging in black sky
men cried, incomprehensible and high

till my thoughts turned and made another world.

Dawn was icy, tender. Calais lay
a smudge at our eyes' edge. Hugh ran to say
when we would land: a stranger, smiling there.
I did not use his name. 'Find me the captain, say
my plans are altered. We will anchor here.'

I thought that he would strike me. I stared back
the unused power: the great eyes blazing black;
the voice blew dawn's blank air. 'We wait for him.'
He shouted in the wind. I turned about
gripping the splintered rail, stiff and salt.

Out of low mist the gold ship rose and fired –
smoke settled low in sun. The sailors cried
gulls whirled – the voices plead. We are surrendered.
They climbed on board. Their eyes turned to a wild

creature of their mind. I only said
'Did you take him?' then 'I am thankful for it.'

They bowed to me. Exemplary and grand
the mistook tide broke over all we planned.

*

He was not cornered in the chartered ship
He was in Holland; gales had blown him there.
My grandmother laughed from some wicked place;
she would have been in Calais, counting sheets.
Mary would have lingered some time there
staring at the sun; until, despair
worked out, she would seek Paris from the port,
to close her fine dark circle in the Court.

Absurd. I wept for days. Slowly I came to see
what might have waited us: the muddy inns;
a woman with bright name but all looks faded.
More brutally, I might have swelled
to meet the septic knife in childbed.

He was my love; but I had played him coldly.
Had he been less young, the howling air
not swept them down the coast, I do believe
he would have turned from land and waited there.
I could not risk them taking him again;
be gracious as the moon
confirm I paid that debt:
Hard as the rail's wood, my memory
escapes me and the emptied hands forget

all but the barren air to which I came.

VIII   *The Tower*

Old tapestry, blown green, like summer leaves
in dreary kindness narrowed more the room.
A high small window let the North light beat
but day died soon; I used to walk
upon the battlements; they rose as cold
as wind on Hardwick's roof; at other times
I walked beside the warder's crusted walls.

God whom I only name, in outer air
the lanes are rushed with light of great spring rains;
white tails of sheep's-wool drip among the briars
moss glitters on the sun's untrodden stone.

Love, your face is gone, in a far air.
I do not think the King will let me free,
I am that risk no State will dare.
Kin crumbles, I remain. This room holds me
not for a day but years of boredom, cold.
Cut in a wall not far from here:
my father's name. I carve no such remains.
A braver woman or a saint might kneel;
in twenty years, James' son may pardon me
what's left; the Court sniffs 'mad', short spring
revives the free, damp eats my body old.

Starvation's not a death I recommend.
At times I float and watch strange colours flow
free as you are; and still more free
could I dissolve – Death's horrible. I burn
and choke on dregs of food. Physicians say
that something else is there; would God grow kind?
Kindness I fear most of all, would keep
Jane from me with her endless steam of soup
beasts' blood. Now I trust Hugh (who planned escape
when first I came, then married, suddenly).

He wraps the pearls (their gold glow soft and deep)
part to pay them, part to buy drugs, for me,

so moons melt black; buy dear, short sleep.

*

Truth must be quick. It may not grieve
that wakeful silent air,
by retching death, post-mortem, more
of body's history – you would not want this.
Say I grew light, take from my sleep
the warm quick pulse by which you live

which beats through time and power
(the tides of language burn)
a word of snow the moon's light
in bitter grace consumes.

Say it was not your eyes I kissed,
say words grow light, and listening cold,
such love beats in this unnamed dust
towards that dreaming power you hold,
stirring, I warn, we wake and must
break cold from dream   find life the ghost.

*

But bitter dust: to write in Mary's book
'your most wretched Arbella' with your name,
and send it you that you might suffer too.
(It is preserved in Russia; do they see
sumptuous fossil, her silk circle; or
beneath the glass the trembled script of pain?)
My dreams still saw you in the window seat –
but holding you, a tall girl with dark eyes –
I was not tall; what longing might reach you?
Yet pain grows lighter, yet I will declare –
I who dreamed you brave when you were young,
that I saw in you truly what you were:
that all men praised you in the civil war
and that your second marriage, the safe bed,
accounts and the deep orchard, could not shut
those clear eyes I had kissed, to misery.
You called your tallest daughter Arabella:
my light name in her, something grew from me.
I ask that girl who walked her mother's orchards,
picked blossom, white unprofitable flower,

had you not realised I was ordinary?
The woman late from work who washed her floor
the man who leaned against the whitewashed wall
stared at the work's black door;
I could not reach to grasp the reins of power;
beside, the horse was bolting; not the strength
but weakness of my cousin's son plunged England
to fighting in white orchards and wet moors.
The age of Queens was over. And my garden
flowers slowly and with ever lower walls;
do you see each man valuable and loved
or truly answer to a common name?
my own faults make me tremble; my mistakes
cry first against me. Only risks are proved.

And our own power known last: the years the cold house closed
unkind and stunted. Still to me
most simple and most strange to understand
is that we do not reach. As I lost you.
Light fills the winter branches, the great sun
beats against the glass and we are there
frozen in love. And love I briefly am
to cry to you in a cold name we pass
as light into bright air and endlessly –

but I died cold: a new pain tore my heart
and none of this at all could comfort me
or wake me as the tide bore down the Thames,
death's flood lets no voice or lover through
strips down the tapestry –
spring's moons explore
the flowers of ice, clear glass,
touch light: wake you.

FROM

Breaking Ground

The Birds

I come back to the students' shabby cloakroom,
To listen to the birds. Their nest is out of sight;
Leaning from windows, in the cool, comes near
Their high dusk crying. Sparrows? no, too sweet.
Starlings? I would not think so. Swallows, yes.
I watch the brown hill shrink. I hear
Sea in their voices, continents of heat.

Rented Rooms

Night stole away my reason to be there –
that routine note which missed the post. I came
out of the throaty mist, the New Year's air,
stared, at the dim house which showed no name,
called to a girl, who rattled past her bike,
blowing her fog-damp scarf, winter's hot cheeks.

The first door I pushed open from their hall
gaped a conservatory, shadowed: full
of spoiled ferns once, sweet geraniums.
Now it held bikes, askew. It breathed back all
the cold of first streets, lingering on stairs –
the outside door blows open – no one cares
to clean: from Christmas, ivy curls in sprays,
dark, in rolls of dirt. Who went away
leaving this television blank above
a rolled-up quilt? Quick: drop the printed note
on the hall's floor.

It echoes back again
the deep sea chill of fog, the waves of dust,
my wonder at a room's dimmed lights.
Need, then:
the stairs to silence; not to own, but love.

Whose Window?

Whose window are you gazing through,
Whose face is stilled between your hands?
The glass glows deeper than your eyes
Where quick lights sink: as feet through sands.

Into your darkness first snow drives,
No soft meander, aimless drift,
But straight as water. Crumbling bright,
Sharp crystals flash, as if they lived.

Now when the great wind throbs the door
When street-light and small hedge are drowned
My face turns open into night.
I am not safe. No, I am found
Melting the hard bolts back. The hall
Is filled with dark air, ice-clouds blow:

A warm face sleeps. I am the snow,
Uncatch your window. Let me through.

Breaking

Something has happened,
something in raw dark
gone between us. Now
the bicycle slips
spinning on air
without power –
chains are easy to fix –

but I,
crouched, for half an hour
in the streetlight's cold eye
drop the broken hedge-sticks,
leave the links meshed hopelessly

begin to walk
through the waves of flu
day held at bay,
to shiver. Click
of the wheel changes,
dragging cracks
of pavements, the children's
the old woman's way
I never tread. Rain flicks. I see

Blossom – drained by the streetlight, pale
it rests on air, a tree whose name
I never learned; half winter's, frail
rain-licked, it gleams.
Now only calm
washes me, a car-lit rain.
The branch is dipped behind my sight
with one, marching, man I meet:
whose spaniel strains the lead: who does not speak.

Once I would have been quite sure
walking to you:
that you, head filled with accidents
would come to find me. 'No.'
I say: as truly 'it is dark'; as perfect tiredness
touched, with petal, weighed with wind
will not resent, feels no distress

but breaks, high flower filled with wind
into a thousand things –
when round the last road's corner swings
the slow car, dull blue as night's sky
when you stare palely at me, I
running to you, thought the rain's blurred glass
will let no sound through, speak your name –
Nothing can happen,
be the same.

Last Week

Last week I had two rows with my superior,
my best friend chose to leave. There was a bomb scare:
we shivered for an hour, among clouds of smoke and daisies
(the smoke was cigarettes, they found no bomb).
I promised next, to strike, risking the dull future –
not the best of weeks, in short. Again the lilac
hangs heavy over other people's fences
and when no one is looking, after rain
I draw the sprays close to me, breathing slower,
brush from my face the cold and vivid water.
The martins have returned, from unimagined seas'
wind-blinded miles, as sudden as they left
their bow of wings, stubbed tails, boldly black
wheel and turn above the crumbling flats;
how tall they make the houses look. The sky
stays further than I thought, further and higher.

Half-day

Padding the green alleys of my grass
Watching jackdaws crest upon the roof
I sit, red dock seed rustling by my head.
Great hollyhocks sway up from last year's roots.

My neighbour's child cries, her mother shouts
'I'm busy with the ironing! You must come in or out!'

So she goes in. And it is sad, the quiet,
The grass still warm, seed-silver. Will she lift
Her face from cloth's slow steam: will she find out
Ironing is duty; summer is a gift?

Apple Country

I am living, quite unplanned, by apple country.
Worcesters come the earliest: sea-green
with darkest red, even the flesh, veined pink.
They have a bloom no hand can brush away
sweet breath made visible. But do not think
to have them through the dark days: they'll not keep,
for that choose Coxes flecked with gold
which wrinkle into kindness, winter's fires.

Where I was born they let no flowering trees
in the bare fields, which grow my dreams, which hold
only the lasting crops: potato, wheat.
How low the houses crouch upon their soil
with fruitless hedges; at the barn's end, cars:

none yours. I have no art for probing back
to such dark roots. Yet if you pass this place
though skies shine lean with frost, no softness dapples
white wall to cave of leaf, yet stranger, knock.

For I will give you apples.

Moving

There is a place where you would always live –
a village; a grey house; a quiet coast
glimpsed for a moment when you were in love,
brimming to the window of a coach
or scarcely seen at all but in all maps
pulsing like a vein into the heart.

The place I saw was Hastings. But in rain
the endless sea is blind.
Where are the tender lights which we saw strung
from the high room we rented, the long slide
men washed down every day? I twist my head,
see rain-green walls. 'For Sale.' So she is dead,

her great jugs ringed with roses; whose man died
oh, years before; what was she, eighty? when
she dragged a new case to us on her stairs,
'for my great-niece; another fits inside.'
That was when she showed us the stripped wall
barred, with dark ships' timbers, bulging bare;
on seas of autumn night I heard them creak –
turned house, turned ship – trying to move elsewhere.

Monday

The air was dark with rain, the day
Held little promise. And I stared
At all the bills, the things to do:
Then I saw you there

In the high room, yawning, staring
At the dull page, in the lamp's glare.

I laughed. Love is not easy, cannot
Will us one or win us time.
Weeks fray us open like a knot.
Worn: all separate: we shine.

Castle

There are lilies in the lake, the lilies of still water
Which part for nodding ducks and close again.
I cannot see my face, they are so close,
Half-opened only, swayed, red stem to stem;
I cross the trembling bridge. Held in the other
Bank, an arch of broken stone pipes gapes
Five silted throats from which no waters fall.
My eye's edge sees – but that would be too strange –
White open mouths of orchids on a wall.

Around the clock is painted a blue heaven
On which the sun's great cycle gilds, and sings.
I cross the yard, bare even of a cat,
Or outstretched dog; or stir of pigeon's wings.
The arches of the yard are white and even
The brass knob of the door is smudged by hands
And I am slower, heavy as the clouds
Which move across the upper sky in pairs,
Now I have reached my certain journey's end
Turning the corner, climbing the closed stairs.

The window is set open and the door
Was never locked. The carpet, once complete
With hunting dogs, tall pairs of gold-chained birds
Is worn down to dark thread, by other feet.
My foot brushes a plate left on the floor
With the dark skins of fruit; fresh apricots
Whose bloom is gone: whose scent would still hang there
If the room were shuttered, closed and not
Open to this sudden cool of air.

I must come here. I must come, many times
Though there is nothing more that I can see
Inside the room or all its passageways
Where small sounds run, too far ahead of me;
No order, day or night, disturbs the chimes.
Yet I may see – if once, I do not watch –
The glint of the stone roof in dark, the moth
Flown before I touch it. I may catch
A hidden breath; the fluttered, warm, black cloth.

Leaving Present

I wonder: what happened to those flowers?
Before a neighbour knocked upon your door
Did you get them into water? If not, they would have died.
So the flower-woman said, screwing up her eyes
Against the light; repeating; they love water.

They were scabious, cool blue. When I returned
I saw them nod, flushed purple, on the hill.
Great butterflies broke up from them, new peacocks
Flashing black wings. The horse reached out to them
Stretching, for a mouthful, but I stopped him.

Untouchable flowers.
To buy them, or to let them die
Is not our end. They rustle through the hands.
They are alive. And what I saw
Came for, is true: the cloud-warm hill: and there
A litter of blue petal, upon your tidy floor.

Leaving

I scarcely notice trains. At our garden's end,
They have become a deepening of the wind
A shudder between voices, or a hum
Rivalling, in my ancient radio
The GI stations and the Russian anthem.
Yawning, in grey air of five o'clock
I kiss you at the station. You are going
To Hungary. I walk the hill streets back,

I do not meet a soul. Scarcely awake
I think of the old cleaner's tales. He took
A train for three days, through Australian plains,
A blue unyielding sky, dry for ten years;
Saw clusters of white houses. Hundreds of miles from rain
From any other men – how do they live?
I miss you; but I do not cry. Each garden
Rustles with birds. The slanting wires give

That peculiar shudder; for your train,
Past the road's dip, where I might have seen
The blue and yellow flash – and you, my face.
I gaze through fences, curtained caravans.
I hear the wheels beat, the cutting race
The sound ahead: until the dull air sings
Without people or clear sky: a grey wide place
Shivering and shadowed, under wings.

Sleep. I must sleep again. Against my chin
Fresh from her fights, the young cat finds a berth.
As bottles clink, the new train draws away –
Letters – milk – your pocket's bread – we sway,
Shaken, in our iron veins, to earth.

Medine in Turkey

'Today' said Hassan – through a mouthful of honey –
'A girl will come who speaks French.' There came
A girl with straight brown hair, her eyes
Flecked with gold, a stiller honey.
Her French was pure and soft. Her name
Was Medine. Her paid study
Ended when her father died.
'Maintenant – j'aide ma mère. Je lis.'

'Je lis Freud,' she ventured, bare feet firm
On the rug's blurred leaves. She lived next door.
Each house leads to a tiny yard
With a dusty tree; white chickens squirm
In favourite hollows. She never saw
France; she sat, this grave brown child
Ten years younger than myself, unmarried
Alight, in their cool best room. She smiled.

There is no answer. Scholarships?
France, too, has hot bored villages
With girls who read all afternoon.
The arranged husband, or their child's care
Will not close up that watchful face
Flecked by lace curtains, endless sun;
Unmoved, she listens for the place
Where the book closes, where the footsteps run.

Brooklands

Between the fast road and the private school
A dark and shaggy hedge takes out the view.
Does water rustle in a garden's fold –
Why else the sprawling name, still slanted blue
Beside the locked door? Was it ever sold?
We could not afford it. But the sale
Brought no one here to live. Viburnums, pale
Tight heads of bud which whiten winter, grow
Glossy, unchecked – a hedge now ten feet high
Lets the front door, blind upstairs windows show.

Late in summer, in surprising heat,
I cycled past through evening, slowly, tired.
Someone had pushed open a high window
An old man sat there writing. As I stared
He raised his eyes: looked calmly back at me.
So they have moved in, at last, I thought.
Next day the long net curtains lay as tight
Across the glass as they had always been;
The door was shut. Was it a neighbour's house
Which I had watched instead? What have I seen?

I do not know. I neither grieve nor care
If someone sorting out their bills, next door,
Had reached and thrust the window up for air,
If it was the surveyor sent at last
To check the rot. The great red dock seeds rust,
The gravel's sunlight, celandines in flower.
The stream runs out of sight. I trust that most
Hearts live haunted. I have seen my ghost.

Toad

Stretched on the road, spread like a hand,
One leg crawling, behind him – I swerved. I was thinking
Of resignation: how I hated
Wet, Friday nights. Now this dead frog:
But it was a toad. As I scooped him out blackness
His pale fingers opened; breath sucked in his sides
He was swollen with anger. He had been crawling
Close to the gutter, in fury of rain
Trusting its stream.

               And where was his pond?
The scoop by the willows the builders were filling?
There is water in one of the horses' fields
In winter, a flood; in summer, a glimmer.
But not to be found in the dark. He was cased
In a high plastic dome, a tray of plants
Sweet Williams or wallflowers; having for water
A plastic dish; and a stone; where he crouched
With only his gold-rimmed nose, still sucking.

I wanted him. What need to be
A prince; with eyes of rusty gold
And brightest black? If I had ponds
With subtle lilies, I would keep him.
But next day, he began to leap
Purposed, silent, launching up
On high back legs – then falling back
Banging the dome, his hidden sky.

We took him through the floating grass,
He was not resigned. Given his stone,
He leapt straight out, splashing and stirring
Dangerous flood, to open sky.
(Two ducks flew, squawking, by our heads.)
He settled then, to his new mud;
His olive back in the drowning grass
His gold eye to the feckless air.

Is he still there? I would not say
That toads are happy, good, or fond
Of their own place; but go for miles,
Choosing their mud, finding their mate,
Until the water glazes ice,
The heron finds the pond.

Bookkeeping

These are not (you understand) the figures
which send cold judgement into the backbone
which leave us, workless, shrunk at home
staring in a sky grown black with leaves.

These are like the ticking of a clock,
the daily sums, a van's new brakes,
three drums of trichloroethylene on the back
of a thrumming lorry; yet they take
a day to make: thin bars of figures. While
I try to balance them, light scurries round
like a glad squirrel. Radio music stales –
until shut off.

          What's left when it is done,
the green book closed? There is no sea to swim
no mouth to kiss. Even the light is gone.
Bookkeepers drink over-sugared tea
lie in dark rooms; are always hunched and tired.

Where I stretch up the low bulb burns and whirls.
And in it, I see him. The dusky gold wing folds
across his face. The feathers' sharp tips smudge
his margins.

Sunk, in his own shadows, deep
in scattered ledgers of our petty sins:
he, the tireless angel:
Unaccountably, he sleeps.

Homecoming

Horses have quick routes they know
A few safe roads, on which they always go,
They are not tempted by the sudden lane
The silver poplar shivering in light.
They only crave heaped hay again,
And pull to keep the low white yard in sight.

So I must fight them, if I am to go
On fruitless roads, on past the dulling tree;
Nor could I tell them, even if I knew
What it was we turned so far to see,
Before the hungry stables of the night.

March Night

The road streams, to the moon. The sky
Is green and solid, lapped by light
The stars are buds, leaf-furled and white.

The children clatter out of dark
Pushing down the stable cart.
'Don't crash it, like you did last night!'

My horse licks out my feeding hand
Stares at the upturned cart, diverted:
The slow moon climbs, behind his head.

As the spilled children pause for breath
Above the broken bread and apples,
Across the sudden fields, sound bells.

I never knew bells which have been
Tumbled, mad, and very sweet
Cast seed so, through a sky's cracked green.

Grooming

Mud hangs its dry beads on your eyelid,
Not on red and glossy hair, but the dark skin
Too tender to be brushed. I hesitate
And then I lick the sponge and touch it to you.
You sigh with pleasure, slip your heavy head
Into my other hand: and let me rub.
Stepping round, stroking your ears, I think
We are too narrow, and our labels
Far too few.
All the loves and all the warmth shut out –
The yard is empty. Finished, like this horse
Who on the hill-top cries for his own kind –
How suddenly, intensely, I want you.

June 21st

I hear you moving softly on the stairs
I rise to follow; it is almost dark;
After the long ride, I smell it, sharp,
The scent of horse on my own skin, as sweet
As their green mouth-froth; grass and seed; a flare
Of speed which does not look, I recognise:
Yet fought today, until my stretched arms ached
'Pull *up*!' The green ground flows – the cliffs end there.

Summer and night – I would ride there again
Washed by rank sweetness of the elderflower
Whose huge, green plates are curled, buds still; to break
To moons. How bare, how high, moons will rise there
Nor show the stones in deep grass, till too late.
No night is safe: but how to hold the light

Escapes you, also? Grounded: I must slide
Lean on the horse's damp hard neck and feel
Us separate. This is the longest day.
Up on the land's green shoulder, barley-sleek
The lovely red-brown of my arms could stay
Close to the sun. Cooler: come home: I lie
Where the grass blows longest, dock seeds, finest,
To thread the sky; a gold snail climbs, its shell
A tiny sun. The stable-cat comes, to rest.
I lift my face up to her; see the sky
Veined with a trace of cloud which does not move,
Feathered with one trail; soft silvered, steel,
The long sky of day's ending: the slow west.

One bare day, will I work? I, who do not believe
In happiness, wake, keeper of small keys,
Reader of books, a rider
Of no man's horses? You my night
I need no hands to touch now: I call moons
To marvel at you, flood your silent gates,
I follow you. Under enormous sky
The horses sleep, together, without sight.

Stone Horse

She is two; with small eyes which see everything.
I like her, as I fear her. She is harder
Than the hundred students in a room
Whom I keep quiet with ease. For she is quiet:
But purposeful. She crosses our rough grass
Where honeysuckle trails, dusked purple, where
The sly fritillaries, blue-leaved like grass,
Watch her with their snake's eyes. She stands by the stone horse.

I stroke its ears, its cream and lavish mane
The collar round its neck – a unicorn's.
She peers into its chiselled face and sighs,
Stoutly impressed. 'Can it open its eyes?'

They are carved open; but in pale stone:
Would she believe those brilliant, icy pupils
The Greeks painted on gods? Or does she think
The head will turn: blinking and bright: alive?

I bend, confused. For I want many things.
'You do not understand. It is just stone,
Come down the road, to see my real horse.'
Or fairy stories. 'When you are asleep,
It gallops through the grass –' You are too good
For such deceit. You felt speed prick its ears;
Shadow quiver, breathe its nostrils, as I did.
You beg to sit astride.

How chill it is
In April's summer. For I sit there too
Blinking in autumn sun, drinking my coffee
Watch something, in its haze. I do not promise, now
A miracle, our hardness will unfreeze
That the stone horse should see – I am about
To take you, kicking protest, to your mother,
Betray you. I say: 'Maybe.'

                    All untrue,
Those eyes shall open: when you want them to.

Mr Street

He praised your shoeing, then your ease
In riding; said, as you were seventy-three,
That you were selling all the horses up.

Gone: as stars scatter. Now I see
Why you worked so hard on me, to buy
Martha, half Irish drayhorse, who would stand
By shuddering buses like a rock; and my
Beloved Joshua; dark, springing horse
With fine and ruined legs. You even tried
Tall Brandy, who could buck me to the sky,
But had him safely sold to someone else.

You were a rescuer. The wilful mare
Who, because a bit had chipped her teeth
Fought every bridle, let you slide hers on.
You had a stout brown pony, thirty then,
Whom you 'kept meaning to put down', but always
Went on; and on. The pied New Forest pony
Hobbled your paddock upon swollen feet
You daubed with healing tar. Who will buy them?

But it is true, the work was heavy. I
Remember as you led them for a ride
After the catching, shoeing, grooming – what
Strange sweat lay on your brow: like a sharp dew
Silvered: a warning. So you heard at last
Your heart's complaint, to outlive horses. Yours

I've heard you number, like a liturgy.
Jumbo, Pepper, Candy, Topper, Patch –
You talked fast as you rode. Can your yard be
Empty? Is your house dark? They have not
Gone. They stand, behind your shoulder. See.

from *Breaking Ground*

I
VISIT

It is no use pretending

this place does not exist;

or saying

there is nothing noble here:
which is true: it is the bottom of the world
the grey sea-bed, where the quick fishes gleam
and turn away. And were there others, once?
we feel, there should be bones: but mud has eaten them.

This place remains too mean to love the dead
or any living thing
admits the day
as pressure of thick water on the forehead –
we do not think to breathe again. Despair
lies several fathoms up. By it, perhaps,
by evening you'll have risen to the dune,
unlooked for as the dead, whose wiry grass
bent dark to wind, scribbles the sand. Down here,
even in this dark, I feel it root:
more beautiful, more sad, than women's hair.

Door's locked. Begin. She yawns,
she has not combed that hair:
I am neater – dead, so unsurprised,
but wish her lovelier as women were,
Mary: young and clear: Patty's long mouth
the gold and broken light across her eyes,
my wide land gone. I tell you who have come
Now all my words are torn, to write me down:

they make porridge here – I sleep; they give me food,
more than the hungry world. My windows tremble iron, my name's
not yours or for your purposes:
                  and each day it will change

                              But ask for grace
who I was, might be: though in my place,
cold as waters froze my roots, you came.

The room spreads – bare as silence – a small table
At which you sometimes write. You face me now:
And I am startled, first, that you are able
To turn so young, lit sudden as a fire
Smile dark – tree shadows glide on boards below.
What ground: what roots are yours? What stubborn glow?

Even to the dark my land would shine:
sharp-rimmed with gold as sun outlines a cloud –
then light soaked through its soil, flowed down each line
to the plough's blade; rising, glittered, showed
horses' clipped manes, warm turning flanks, slow steam;
cracks in the skin of leather: love
was lit in small things, I believed,
the goldfinch tossing tiny in the wind
the kingcup's yellow splash by flooding stream.

In winter we ran headlong to the cold
which numbed our fingers quickly; we would leap
on great sheets of white along cart-tracks
to feel the ice crash, the black water break
gurgling and free. The frost-ruts stubbed our toes.
Hare and hounds we played through parishes,
stumbling home through dark, saw none too soon,
bright as our scraped plates, the famished moon.

So I was bound upon the seasons' wheel.
And truly, I do not remember pain
except of falls; unworried hunger; then
I did not have to plan. The sun, so new,
a miracle to slant my sleep, became
familiar: dull and weary as a drum,
beats endless winter I cannot turn from.

III
ON THE BOARDS

I turned a boxer: although short;
with my great drive to the jaw
each time I fought I laid my man
cold, on the bare white board.

So I grew known at country fairs:
And all the boys ran after me.
Young women raised their children high
That they might turn, and see.

Then dukes and earls paid all my fare
That I might go to London,
But when I left the warm coach there
I saw a sky made stone.

In high lit rooms, I drank white wine
which let my tongue strike quick,
Cut glass rang stars, deep carpet lay
Red as my blood and thick;

but when I came back late that night,
all rooms were dark, none home.
No man I knew in all those miles
To give me bread or room

Then I walked home: and lost three fights:
and was despised by men
who fed me porridge and raw meat
To have me fight again.

     But He with eyes remote as stars
Reared up to twice my size
With one great blow, He split my head
     and so I sank and died.

The village shutters closed at noon.
The children, with bare feet,
to the crying of my bell
ran out along the street

93

and filled the church and stood in rows
to watch the coffin pass
and on the bare and boarded box
cast every flower there was,

marigolds of sun and flame
light stocks as sweet as women's love
briar roses, frail as wrists of girls,
with every thorn plucked off –

because I faced the sun for them
and cast the dark shapes down
still they will sing me, warm and free,
though I am locked in ground.

o mad, quite mad. He had some short success,
was asked to London; treated kindly; but
nature fell from vogue; books failed; he wrote
stranger. Stranger: in and out of time
to wind and the great dark: to men's cold eyes
for whom? to no one? does he square:
Before me in this bare, white room
Torn scent, strange flowers, crowd the air.

V
ENCLOSURE

Look down –
you ride the cold air, as he dreamed,
but cannot rise so far
as the white mounds of cloud-floor, the high and breathles
that blue he dreamed: not saw.
Chill trails, low mist part round you. Peer and see
a moor; a waste; stretches of green and grey
marked by faint tracks, rough slopes where great trees star
small cattle, like dark grain, watched by a boy
or an old man – no hedge, wide road to break
this land of mist, space: silence. It was England
unenclosed. That space was never ploughed.
Slow in the uncut grass my skirt sweeps dark,
my feet start up deep dew. New mushrooms here
burst warm, as white as flesh – did it once seem
the fields were mine? sleep-walking as mist cleared,

                    I drove sharp furrows miles,
till waves of mud upon my strong boots weighed
and clogged me: but on land we worked each year.
The commons' grass was greener, tense with time,
with flowers, you could not now dream: the brief
orchids' dew-white glistening mouths. I knew
each sheltered tree; their deep roots bound my life.
To see that free land broken by the plough:
it was as if men cut my body through.

'There was a time when every elm tree died,
not in one place, but thousands. They were burned –
People took fear at it; as though the fire
which crumbled bark to ash, marked their own end.

Is there no strength in us: to ride, past change?
England lay forest once –'

You speak too narrowly.
You speak like them.

                    He kicks a rotting stump,
woodlice shower from it, over lumps
of creamy wood: they scramble, to get free.

Think what you saw: the cattle, sent to feed.
Whose were those pastures? They were common land;
all he had, that herd-boy, running down
behind a milk-cow, stamping at the cold.
The tracks lay anyone's. You walked all day
and never saw a fence. But part by part
the wild ground was divided; shut away
hedged by its owners' shadow: a rich land, without heart.

I think of building-sites, how they glow good
and warmth to winter: where the fires pull
their stubborn blue in wind: the handled bricks grow walls;
sweet through wet air you smell sawdust, dry wood.
But when smooth tiles are fixed and people come,
when builders fill their vans and disappear:
then with their shouts and roof-top whistles, gone,
strange silence rides on air:
dark, woven fences, ruffed gold flowers in rows
which are not let to mix or seed
        Enclose. Enclose.
He picks white bramble-flower clustered low
one pink – to twist them through a buttonhole.
The fruit glints black, looks sour – from frost, so soon?
He lopes, half-gipsy. Would he understand
deep towns or us: shut in them, patiently?
His light is open land.

How is your county?

'Rich,' I say, 'well-drained,
The fields are huge: skies sweep them, stunt them; now
no drifts of cowslips as my father found,
their throats splashed red; the sows live penned, inside.'

And the enclosure –

                    Once I drew its map
a child's crayon fields; remember, squelching black
unkind fruit; frosted: nothing sweet but seeds.
'The Earl of Scarborough built a carriage road –
whose cost, with hedging, fell upon all those
with any land; the poorer people sold
their ground to pay the debt. How much they owned
I cannot tell you; for they walked its measure
in strides too small for sense now: 'perches', 'rods' –'

What I arraign is not the broken mist.
We had illusions, better without them:
perhaps – Nor will I halt and name again
the plants, the paths I loved, which they destroyed.
Listen; leave that fruit. Those men did this
with shut and unkind hearts, and for their own.
What happened to those people of your village
who sold ground to meet the Earl of Scarborough's claims?
Ask your great-grandmother, broken: young. But you –
whose eyes are blurring in the glow of mist –
I know your cities. They are fortresses.
They shut out light and care. Round all of us
there is a poorer world than England was
your open world – Behind your painted doors
you hide: and all you spare falls less,

than scraps, we fed to pigs. Unclosed as day
my torn mind blows and shifts – till I forgot

if you own God? Name one: so you may say,
he pardons you. I have none. I do not.

from VI
BREAKING

You smile, quick audience I scarcely know:
turn again, your skin drawn tight, as now
believing little: sensing much –
black, new space.

                You stole your closing line.

'Would you have known as much, in life?' I say.

I walked ten miles, buying a first book,
to read my 'poet'; who has taught me, what?
call rough, white water 'silver', be unsure
of raw sight; broken stick, trapped in the stream.
Colours, which glow new-peeled: jays' cries, air blue
tear the wood's mist; still reach me. But before
only the stories: ghosts, and witches: mere
bogies, frightened mind. My sense lay starved.

'Could it think our rooms rich? whose stronger light
might make you flinch; smooth carpet masking floors;
a glowing square where coloured lines might show

anything: new worlds?'
                   as to my tall
grandfather – fire sun-red, he sat late
gazing in those pictures; curled pipe-smoke
tender and incredulous round his chair
he watched skies open – silver, dancing men
drift in the soft moon dust: treading air.

'Don't trust: it shows you other gleaming rooms
all you might own, strange tricks to make you fear,
new bogies. Walk into its room, at night,
and a cold, shut silence fills you there;
the lightless air – Yes: I live so; work
and skim through papers, on the brink of sleep
through bombs and prizes, shiver and forget;
and next day in the slow rain, sleep to work.
So, now, we starve: so richly that we lose
kindness – which is space: enclosed, enclosed.
We make, and buy: but never own a voice.

Yet you spoke? I will tell you: do not flinch,
that your words are not torn, they are still read.
Is there no warmth in this, to comfort you?'

If the warm voice spoke true –
not late, no – but too soon:
How many read? yet write my trust. I still
will speak unspoken pain: what I was then:
The hawk drives down from emptiness to kill.
The land is brutal: you should know how hard.
The thin cats fight for scraps in the grain-yards,
dogs are beaten. Walking, I would see
thin rows of twine stretched tight across a tree,
my stomach caught with sickness; they were hung
with weasels, twisted, dancing, mouldered skin;
with black crows shot to pieces. Men would say
'the keeper does this, to keep pests away;'

the killing is inside us. Clear autumn saw – ah, what
would you call it, my season? the trusting sow's throat cut.

Then they gave me allowances, they said
You will have time to write. But not enough.
She worried for the children; then we moved
To Northborough, the fens, damp, low and dark.
I scarcely slept. I could not write at all;
I had no strength to bind again the small
things I have told you of; goldfinches; gleam
of frost in air, as winter dammed all streams.
One night I woke, choked with black breath and fear
and still by Patty's side, ground on the quilt
with empty hands; lest I should cry to her.

Yet she returned. What did I say, before?
You must not think her beautiful.
Her teeth were pointed, her quick mouth too long –
her smile not that perfect outer light
but flaring, deep, inside. I felt, not saw,
her turning to me, in the empty room,
her hand warm round a book I had not read.
From then, I felt, I knew:
though I could not admit: that she was dead.
Only the dead are easy with us, smile
will never cheat

                do you think yet, or guess
that links may come between us, fine as silk
which stretch and bear for ever: cannot break?

'I . . . I would believe so,' having found
songs he wrote for Patty, after years
in the asylum: naming her: still kind,
green and secret as the unfenced land.

But she did not come often. I took spades
to that sad ground; and stopped; mocked by the sun

in my eye-corners. I was gone
in days, to silence, over angry fields.

'They certified you mad.'

With reason: as I slopped their thin grey food,
I was, too soon, the earth. I chose too late:
a husk of dark: but throbbing through me rose
cool orchids' mouths, white foam of cuckoo flower.
I slept for seasons. Night's room filled my head;
flashed past the constellations, autumn skies.
Behind the steady Plough, swift Pegasus,
the harvest's homeless stars glowed in my eyes.

Where is she gone? She has laid down my pen –
the living rise too quick! crosses white boards,
traces my name on glass, where her mouth blurs

orchards – mist light as bird:
breath flickers, comes

Wait – I am not Clare:

                    who once, I loved,
or her, with pale loosed hair. I saw no choice.
Called into closed space I turn, my voice
echoing last light between them both
bent to the sill (strange visit's end) they watch
bullfinches: scattered apples in frost's branches.
He whistles through high glass. They glow, take flight;
the hazed sun, chill rose, in the webs of white

where light is fear. Laid in the low sick room
my torn head aches; so, stubborn, I would sink

in the dark root, the silence, but there's none.
The broken stars rise in us

                    the low fire
mutters, is the wind, is all I hear;
him ill, I cannot write, no, not his name.
I stare through light: soft gold, flames tire
tremble through young twigs. Come –

see, torn love, whose face
turns tender, half-lit fields,
how strong a kindness flares beneath desire:
enclosed as the blind fire
holds heat: here in
                    a shuttered room ash quivers
                    the hawk, the lark's white sun.

                    Sunk from whirled flight, from fear,
                    Her hand burns silver: lies.

I wake untouched. My cold lips ache,
I yawn, brush black hair, sing.
Deep in March root wind turns,
dark woods glow. Riding, free,

the broken ground, your dust, breathes;
earth kindles air; love sees.

FROM

Christmas Roses

Crewe to Manchester: December

When I was here last, foxgloves foamed the banks,
moon-daisies were dipping. I repeat this:
I cannot believe it. All I can see
is brambles' dark smouldering, quelled by the rain.

Where is the skewbald pony who wandered
field ridges in sunlight? The cattle seek high ground,
small ponds sweep in flood. It was a wild night –
even the angler tramps back over fields,
his stream's swell too high to be borne.

Why did I wake
at three in the morning
wholly convinced it was dawn?

But my daughter; I wish you could see my daughter
Stretch woolly hands to an Alsatian,
The blunt pale claws scrabble her coat
Flourish their mud down her prim coat.
She calls to the white cat when she wakes,
Is not afraid.

        Softly you say –
Glancing to the empty window –
She is ignorant, not brave.

Say that there was not a time
We walked through branches with the beasts,
The stars rose: we were not afraid.

Now in our winter we can see
A child scanned before its birth.
Silver fish on a dull screen
Kicking up, out the black stream,
Where have you gone?

Lolled back, she sleeps
In the icy sun, the moss-green pram,
Still with her arms held stiffly out
The wings of a swan. So Cygnus flies –
They tell me – through the winter heaven;
I cannot find him from my book.

That we must, still, be told, then look,
Forcing old lines round fleeing light,
Is that your way? I tremble, see
Bright Castor, Pollux, held and free;
Lovers, beasts, who once they were
Does not disturb them, constant pair.

Look back, past me. White streams of sky
Wheel over; I stand, trying
To track lost stars this night. She was not
Swimming. She was flying.

At Night

Sometimes, awake, she did not cry,
stand, and rattle at cot-bars
but called out lightly, reaching far,
to see if you or I might come
press down the darkness with a thumb
unblind blue curtains; show behind
her black trees buck in gales of wind.
Once, when she turned to sleep again,
I heard behind my closed eyes' glare –
though she lay still; though no one came –
a slow voice sang to silent air.

Visiting Martin

'That little horse did breathe on me.
I still have that warm breath.'
The Shetland licks you. People have
shut him, small white lion, in sheds
but they have always brought him hay.
He has no time for fear.

Stand back – The she-Alsatian bounds
at his soft belly. See him kick
hard, precisely. Guard yourself!
The dog looks thoughtful. He trots on.

You and the stable's child can ride
the crumbling haystacks, packed and green.
Under the iron roof's cracks you view
the dipping fields. 'I'm looking out
for lobsters,' he cries. Carefully,
as the bruised dog, I ask, 'Have you
ever seen one?' 'No,' he says.
Sprightly, ''course not! They live in seas.'

This is a sea, of animals
stacks, crested mud. But I am cruel:
should flash you up to the hard air:
where television glimmers pink
with plastic ponies. To playgroups
all the dry girls carry one.

Well, you can sink. Or you can swim
one eye on the electric sun
one on the sifting depths. There is
no sure land where your home is.
At three, you still hold that warm breath:
you still want plastic ponies.

Cinders

The great clock strikes: once only! Never again
will small feet go scuttling down the stairs,
the hem unravelling, softer than the flick
of the grey rat's tail. Hair tumbles down
unpowdered, dull. She is as far from home
as from a deck the land-lights slide away.
'As she ran back' – a calm voice says, 'You know:
she should have taked the prince with her.'

                                               The dress
is neither sack nor silk. It is the blue
of stormy summer, in the almost dark.
The hedgehog snuffles peacefully. He sees
no ribboned mice, no bare feet, nor the slime
of the rotted pumpkin; in his night
the prince stays, but the clocks strike all the time.

Going to Malvern

I think we are lost. In Tewkesbury
by the river's houses, gilt with sun
I guessed a turn, then swooped to stop
in a council estate. Long, rusted cars
swept past to work, though it was Saturday.
With hazy eyes, in drowsing light
I scanned my map, then drove away
down the wrong road. Five miles on
we reached the rich land. There my friend
lives islanded by gardens. Her dog has feathered paws,
clematis tumbles down her trees like stars.

'Never mind!' you call, from the child-seat,
in a trance of content. From Tewkesbury
the true road to Malvern is wide and lush
fat ponies graze, chained to the verge, slow tractors
trundle wet muck. You sing, then as you halt
I cry again 'I think that we are lost'.

For I cannot see hills, for constellations
of the commons' dandelions. I blink
through shine of glass, the mist of sky. It parts
to a rock wall, sheer fall of night, the hills.

Out of the wasted years, a man dreamed there
night's angel spoke to shepherds and to poets:
to shepherds first. Wrapped in his sleep's rough clothes
he watched the poor men swarm across the plain.

I tell you this, buy you a hill of ice-cream
in shabby rooms above the Abbey's gate.
The waitresses, bored children, eye the street's rush.
He had one child: Colette, a pretty name.
No one tells us her dream: of fairer hair?
a kinder father?
                          On the Abbey lawns
boys carry folded banners to new cars.
They frown into the sun. Under this rock
another, shut in warm rooms, brooded day
till soldiers stamped the beat of his loud music,
which does not light the girls' eyes or give time
to those who rest in deep dry grass of summer.
It folds its colour in a narrow space.

I drive the broad road quickly, while you nod,
for I exhaust you, with my awkward strength.
My grandfather brought lambs home; coming later
I touched the angel. I have given you
a foreign name, a mound of white ice-cream.
What will you do –?

                          That is the dream,
of faded silks which age the light. To break
new speed to kindness, lost at every turn,
old hills rear up: dark hills past Malverns. Wake.

On Midsummer Day

I have heard their voices, from a country
shaken by tractors, burdened by empty rooms:
where small apples fell untasted in the gardens.

They did not come at Hallowe'en, in the blind rain.
In the broad heat of June they walked from the wood
where dog's mercury huddled in poisonous crowds.
As at rest from work, they sat on the field's margin
with hay heaped green, its flowers still to finger,
gilt of buttercups, purple dust of heartsease:
small pansies starred more open than their faces.

Beneath thick skirts and hems I saw their boots
pale with dust of summer, turning tender feet
of men and women rough and burning.
I knew that they had tramped round farms for work –
now the towns flood people –
that the apple tree, self-sown,
dropped misshapen bobbins, soft and tasteless.
House walls still run with damp. What can be new?

'As I came to the wood, wheat broke,' I said,
'into white ripples from a sound. They hung
red signs upon the gate which cried out "Danger!"
I heard a shotgun blast among the trees.'

'There was always shooting in the woods,' they said.
'If we had guns we would have shot there too.'

So the gap fell between us, the old shadow,
Raw and new. A gun boomed, far away.
Out of the hot June evening, the air trembled.
Rain would come. White willows at the wood's edge
Flick red silence.

'Just before you came,
out of wild grass, red docks, flowered nettles' –
I spoke of nothing, but to keep them there –
'a dragonfly flashed by, its wings pure black.
Its body shook light-blue. Then snowy moths,
all foreign creatures from the shortest summer.'

'Yes.' Eyes creased, they nodded.

'Do you mean
that you have seen it? But you are my people
from the flat land's blank corn –'

'There were still woods.'

'But it was never there! Just now, I came
alone up this broad slope through whitening stalks
where quick wings came; then left me. You were dead.'

The guns fell quiet. Wings shivered, thin black heat.
'Look. Here is the dragonfly,' they said.

Wood Pigeon

If you have seen winter flocks fluffed in park trees
Soaring the plundered acres of corn
You must think pigeons large. Shot, it was small
In the dead grass by the laneside wall
It crouched, as if nesting, eyes perfectly bright.

The sky, the cloud-moon sharpened for frost.
The wood held its foxes, the guns broke the wood
Cracking in volleys. It heaved tangled wings:
Its eyes still shone. Had I driven a car
I could have taken it, if I had walked
I could have carried it carefully home.

But I was on horseback. My rough, heavy cob
Snorted and snapped, almost stamped on the bird.
I set out to walk, pigeon crooked in my arm.
I saw no wounds or blood. Then the horse smelled the guns,
Leapt from me, danced at the end of his rein.

Sharp as a dream, the untroubled sky
Where rosy clouds streamed, where the flocks had gone,
Flew chill and clear over. The horse, steaming heat
Heaved as I mounted, eye glinting for home.
His trot shook the bird. Does silence fold pain?
Once, as he bounded, the soft pigeon fell
From the jacket's poor hold on the hard saddlebow.

I opened my coat in the quiet second lane.
The slim head turned to me, with berry-black eyes.
Still I hoped for it, yet feared it would smother.
As it slid down against me claws scrambled, wings beat.
Then I fought with my horse for a second hard mile
Past elder, past stubble, frost glinting on walls.

But the pigeon lay still. Mistrusting, I looked.
Its beak gaped half open, its eye, twilit grey.
It had died as it struggled, back in the high lane.
So I let it fall in the fox's white grass
A chilling bundle; at last, let the horse
Storm into canter by moon-rising home.

114

That, filled with lead shot, it had waited in quiet,
That the live horse should fight me, indifferent and hot
Stand glad in his stable, snatching his hay:
I wondered at none of these things.
Yet death surprised me. It was wild,
A falling, an opening of wings.

The Lane

I do not remember the name of the lane.
Bent like a dog's hind leg, it ran
Behind two villages; at the joint came
To a concrete bungalow where a thin dog
Danced on its chain, where sometimes a man
Called it off, rough as a voice through the fog.

Caudell? Northfield? Somersby? No.
I can say, at the far end, rose a wood
Whose violets crept through pine-needles, so
Short-stemmed it was hard to pick them. Then
Came the sudden hill, where my legs and heart stood
As they burst; to the clank of a bicycle chain.

I should not have gone there alone; and yet
The only place where I stood afraid
Was the emptied cottage, where the wet
Rose scrambled nettles; where inside
Faint flowers left mould; beyond, the pond;
In which I thought some miracle must hide.

Only young rabbits appeared, scenting dusk,
Who were not certain if they were afraid,
Sat frozen for long breaths; then gave me up.
They flicked fringed ears, then turned back instead
To untrodden grass, to red bramble-leaves, played
In glimmered hedge-tunnels, nodding their heads.

After belonging, I strained to go free.
I have seen tawny foxes, springing down walls,
Met the owl's wide stare in the winter tree.
Only in sleep, I pass down there again,
Hear the dog's chain sink, the rabbits' feet pause,
The light stems snap – You walked with me there, once.
Do you remember the name of the lane?

On the Move

They made no sound, then very close
Came a rush, like wind. 'Jump on the gate!'
The old man called. The boy stared down.
They poured below, a sea of rats,
Still made no sound, no twittering,
As starlings who in their high clouds
Darken snow-fields. Purposely,
Ignoring men, the rats swept on.

So said the boy, the truthful man,
My grandfather. I know no one
Alive who saw such things. Then say
The rats belong to hungry time.
Today, below December's sun
Wind whistled through an elder bush.
My skin crept tense. I heard the rush:
Saw, on a bare road, two rats run.

One fled, a foot long, but its mate
Smaller, turned on the broken verge.
The stacks held bait. Perhaps too late
Or in their cool and perfect wit
To seek another shelter out,
They vanished through an open gate.

Where is our hunger? All you see
Are corn-filled barns, for miles around.
Beside the broken elder bush
Listen: though you hear no sound.

Grey Velvet

No one I knew had a velvet dress,
With nap as fine and dense as mole's,
Which fell across worn neck or wrist
As snow fills ruts and holes.

Was it a once-used evening bag
Seed pearls clouding down its rim:
An old cape, from a village sale,
Moth-laced inside the hem?

Greyer than mole's cheek, than the sky,
Whose was this dress? I know
It came last night, before I slept,
And lay on me like snow.

Fox and Hounds

You will never come close to the fox. Even in summer
He breasts the cream wheatflowers, ginger
As cat: sees you at field's edge,
Like wind, is gone into the hedge.

With winter grey along his face
He streams across the hill to race
The thin wheatblades. After a long
Pause of sky, the white hounds come.

They scramble, smaller than you thought:
Their tails whip. Their throats have caught
Out of the mud, a chime so high
It beats the clouded, empty sky.

Bewildered, they sniff through the village for scent.
They claw the shed door where the old cat went.
Whipped up; whistled; they trot through night's
Quiet lanes; wait bunched at traffic lights.

The fox's hole bulges, with earth and stones,
Gripped between tree roots. Its cold is the ground's.
The dogs swim deep in a sea of straw.
It will always be warmer to run with the hounds.

Blue

They are peacock blue.

They lift their wise ears,
their eyes are calm.
They lie in the dips
by the breast of the walls

They are sheep.

The dye of the herd numbers ran
smudged by the incessant rain
harsh blue folds the ewe
frail blue folds the lamb
fine as a woman's clothing.

They are warmer than
the rinsed-out sky.
They are brighter than
the lichen's grey.
They will all go for slaughter.

Do not feel pity for the lambs
it spreads like dye
too deep –
it opens dams
to incessant rain
it is impossible
as the blue sheep.

Hawthorn

May stinks. Why do we like it so?
For its rust of buds, as last snow strikes at hills,
For freckled, opened white which spills
Down dull lanes, shines to clouded skies,
Because it is early summer. So
The season I married, ten years ago
I walked through a town I longed to leave
Down by the river; heard evening breathe,
The swallows swish low. Now, I thought
All things may happen, from this day:
I was right, oh and wrong, sweet stink of the may.

Grace

Need, need, need. The soft grey stones
Were laid in gates for carriageways.
This western town needs silly money,
Weightless frocks for summer time.
By shabby doors the stones have sunk.
Dodging new puddles from my road
I see the low sky ripe with cloud.

Where I grew, there lived a woman
Who taught in Chapel Sunday School.
She and the preacher had 'affairs'.
Her long gaunt face passed me by while
We sat around our work's long tables
Slipping forms in envelopes.
The women in their sky-blue clothes
Talked of children, chimed in jokes.
One spoke of the East Coast. I said
Half a sentence of the flood –
This was checked, gently, as too dark.

In storms in nineteen fifty-three,
Some months from my birth – the sea
Rushed down small streets at dykes and farms;
It drank her baby from her arms.
Ten years on, with two sons, still
She would cry at the slightest thing.
The neighbours sighed, then only half
Censured flight from heavy preaching.
Grace was her name. Town roars; I tread
Pavement as bare, as smooth as palms.
Her dark eyes close. Where traffic ebbs
She leaves her light weight in my arms.

School Dinners

Why do I dream now, of people from school?
I am not old. They are not dead.
Yet warm before waking they surface, thin,
or in Janice' case, still fat.
                                    She dyed her hair
in red rats' tails; thought brash. She hitched her skirt,
her wide thighs wobbled. She was kind as silk.
One day, chattering, tipped salad cream
over her favourite pudding;
                                    did remember
to ask the boy's address, but found it false.
They left the seaside camp. She had a daughter,

who now, I think, must be the age
of Janice in my dream; when giggling still
she reached out for the cheap gold-coloured jug.

Eight people made that table. Who do I still know?
No one who could tell me how she lives,
cooking great Sunday dinners? married? happy?
My ignorance stays perfect as the moon
dropped, like a coin through a barley field,
drowned, in all the blue waste of the sky.

Sitting by my daughter in a car
borne smooth and cool, through tunnelled trees
it strikes me, quick as shivering; that when
they must end, yet I will see them there
small and clear, in the battered jug,
their mistakes; their tails of red hair.

Produce of Cyprus

Picking grapes from a paper bag, sucking the misted skin
I think of the island which grew them, Venus' ground
(the rain is in sheets on my window, wet, green, blind)
there, the dry song of the cicada, there the warm nights
with the window propped open, sea's stripe on the counterpane.

Yet they too, have their troubles. The frosts were late;
the land does not love us, relentless stony ground
though we own it down generations. The price of grapes
is falling; and so on. No doubt they dream of us
that far and prosperous country; on its window, the wealth of
    the rain.

The last is tough. The bag, as I put by the rest
rustles and whispers, Paradise is the place
of which we know nothing, which we know best.

Moths

Out of the dark the moths come, beating
Against ungiving plaster, waiting
Folded in our breathing rooms.
As they stay – quivered – you may look
To match their patterns to a book
The scarlet thread, soft black in thumbs.
Though by next morning they have gone
Still they are clear, remembered, tame,
While, pale and sudden, new wings come
Whirl from the glass, and leave no name.

Brocklesby Mausoleum

The air was still, and very hot
For May. I sat beside Eileen,
My then best friend. The slow bus stopped.
We saw a dome through the village trees:
The mausoleum, on whose cropped slope
Sheep droppings gleamed like liquorice.

Eileen, who had sharp brown eyes
Flashed with laughter at a card
Pinned to the great doors, which advised
We find 'Mrs Jackson' – who lived, simply
'Under the Buckle': heraldic stone
In a cottage wall. She found her key,

She was quiet and large, blinked at the sun
As we, inside that dome, at dark:
Tall white shapes, in hard marble. One
Was Sophia, Countess, who crossed
Plump ankles (not unlike Eileen's)
To stare at us, as favoured dust.

The inlaid walls ran veined, more blue
Than the raised eyes of the thin
Boy I burned to meet, but who
Met Eileen, on the Paris trip.
Then we walked home, snapped violets in
A frail wood by a rubbish tip.

As she left school but I stayed on
As I still brooded on the boy
Eileen wrote but only once,
Her family moved: vanished. But she
Who loved soft clothes, warm kitchens, grew
So bored, I heard, she joined the Army.

This night, two hundred miles away,
May's winds turn mad. They strain to lift
The stiffest trees, till as I lie
I think I hear them fly the streets,
To drop, in lulls, upon a drift
Of black, washed earth, to force new roots.

The boy was vain; but you were quick;
You laughed; you would not trust the past.
Tomorrow, though the lion winds lick,
I must go out. I will not take
My time again in days so still,
So hot. Eileen, are you awake?

Snow Queen

Do you remember the Snow Queen story,
Not in a book, but a cartoon film?
Having tea with our cousin, whom we did not like,
We watched it half-heartedly, dull grey and white,
But the Queen wore the silver of midwinter night –
Transfixed, I watched her while you played.

There is that longing to come to the edge
To walk in the blind and dazzle of snow
To scramble to hills' crests, although the night presses –
Can I touch it in you, if you do not know?

Remember instead, that small boy who ran
Too close to her coach and was carried away;
Patient with our cousin, the gas fire glowing,
Did you not notice? Then you will not know
What she had done first, to hold him apart;
The crooked light, shining from eyes I met later,
The shiver of ice inside the heart.

Wasting Time

Certainly, you could clean the house better,
Do the ironing, get your papers up to date,
Chase promotion. Wait – What is that shrilling
From the plantation, where the sea of nettles
Keeps even children back?
                                    A blackbird hurls
At nothing I can see; at air? a steep
Stump of white, and rich brown; an old tree?
Come close. Look down. It is an owl, asleep.

Storms shook our night. They would have slowed his flying,
So he was overtaken by thick day
So he became this bush. Tall as a baby
His claws can lock him still against the winds,
The mobbing blackbird, though his head has turned
Above his back, to feel the road. His eyes
Blink without opening, all the long face shivers.
Watch him for an hour: would you see
Shadows of racing white: winds of the moon?

You have too much to do, just as the bird
Whirls against its small air, black and slim.
The owl does nothing, but claw mice, then
Grow still as a tree. You can do without him.

During the Ideal Home Exhibition

Is that white line, swans, with sky's wings smudged
By river oil, by the bridge's shadow?
No, this is London, never trust:
They are plastic floats: which dipped, and fell,
To beat of breath, bound to a barge
Which rears from mooring, swell on swell.

My coach slides by. The people patter,
Dwarfed by red banners of 'Ideal Home'.
They push bored children who nurse their litter
Of cards, free gifts. Small window's space
Writes 'Rooms – Own Key'. White houses curve,
Policemen tie tapes, as for a race.

It is the man, the 'Earl's Court Gunman' –
Who shot a barman, far away,
Escaped. Now, cornered in a van,
He has lived one day. Although the wide
Air dropped to ice, his darkness stinks,
He grips his own gun, crouched inside.

The street is passed. Red, wet, gates swing.
Soon – he must – he will clamber down,
Drop the warmed gun; like smoke, be gone.
'Vacancies'. By a basement, boots,
Carpets, haired lino, wait through rain
To grow green mould, seed grass, make roots.

Night muttered, You? Are you afraid
Of being caught? Sleepless, he might
Break out, blaze bullets down the road.
Light brought a fresh shift, who instead
Lobbed riot gas. Choking on dark
The gunman shot through his own head.

The vans filed past. A woman came –
Middle-aged, no one he knew –
Who set a bunch of tulips down,
Red wings, the barman's face, his own.
The tips blew black above the pavement,
Waterless. She too went home.

There is no prison where he lies
In blankets stained by other men,
Watches a light blank out the day,
Clenches a hand, without its key,
Listens to feet; police, warders, go
To boxes, home; whom he calls free.

Spinner

The spider walks across the air
He curls a long foot round his thread
His legs, brown-striped in sunlit grass
Jerk, as wakened from the dead.

So I; at last released from work
Can sit beside the unwashed glass,
See the slow spider stalk through space
Until a green half-hour has passed.

Then, as he twists and firms the thread
There swerves in me this sudden joy
Although his lightness turns a trap
Though all he makes there, will destroy.

Hips

It is the last day leaves shall smell of summer –
a great wild rose-tree slants above my path,
sways hips of liquid red.
No bird has torn at them for seeds,
yellow, downy. Scarlet shines
a glass not skin: too smooth for fire.

Below, lie footprints of the hunters,
mud through which they churned and turned;
not only rich blood, chasing blood,
but the decorator's daughter
high on a hired horse.

There is hunger in the North.
Fire crackles in their streets.
The people who were fed with things grow bare.
Their strike's roots spread; find winter.

In the mild South, whose long grass smokes with pollen,
cloud scarcely breathes, I turn at last
to meet them on a road which no mud hides,
a street which grew no roses.

– there, as the paper burned, I saw your name
and mine; and others; and the pictures too
the girl's raised hand, the bird's bright eye
free as the raw air, flickered –

What are they, uncounted fruits
the gales drive down, the black frosts shrink
birds drop in any crack –
                            are these our seeds?

Woken

They have cut the tops off the grass.
The prisoners say, the seed
Will return its airy head
And plant the world.

Sometimes the prisoners see
Not awake – turning –
A face which passes for a moon:
A woman burning.

There are no prisoners here.
Some time in the night
There was a hand which found my face,
Careless as you, as light..

Perhaps

Perhaps it is like
Walking from town, on a hot day,
When shopping drags your hands to the floor,
Your clothes are rough with sweat
You wonder why you bought these things? Flecked white
Dances the pavement, the sharp shore. Hard light
Closes your eyes, like blinds: and then
You see the high wall with its shade, where a dog
Might lie on its paws and sleep, through the heat, the heat.
You stop: begin to cross.

Collection

I have been round the bungalows again
I hate them like the shaking grip of flu.
Even their lawns are shaved too close
with white and broken grass. Their earth holds rows
of parched bright marigolds a daughter came
to thrust in hurriedly one afternoon.
Then the rich groundsel sprang no back could bend
to pluck – No, in my hurry I confuse
the formidably neat, who still wear hats
skewered on straight; the wild, who slam their doors,
who talk to no one but those 'relatives'
who hold keys which, reluctantly, they use.

Halls smell of hot dust on electric air,
of one continual fire; of old paint,
a ghost of cabbage or of liquorice.
I edge from the glass door when shapes appear
I wave my envelopes and try to smile.
Do I rob them? Not all the old are poor,
some keep long cars, curtains in glinting folds.
My daughter in her vivid pink coat sleeps.
Unhelpfully, the round is for 'the old'.

Next year, I swear, I won't go back again.
My feet are burned by steps. My eyes are sad
from all that dull paint. Yes, I am afraid
not of the feebleness that is the old –
the slack wrists – but their fierceness, to scold
me for my daughter's sleep, the reckless wind.
But two at least came radiant to see us.
I breathe their garden's air, I hear them call
to each other: where red wallflowers burn, to touch
blue larkspur. Held the aged. Help us all.

Temperature

My head's the axis. I am turning, turning.
My feet make a compass through starry water.
The sun is spinning inside my eyes.

'Are you going to die?' asks my daughter, robed
On the hairdresser's stool in a long rose gown.
Gravely she watches dark hair snipped down.

My eyes are the axis, turning, turning.
The sun is spinning, like you, my daughter.
Out of the compass of my head
My feet are crossing the starry water.

Off the Road

Where the trees ended and low bushes crouched
Where a white dust road turned down from the tarmac,
There, in the wind of dusk, the oryx stood.
Tall as a man, thick horns thrown back,
Barred with bold black, they watched, then ducked
Around: plunged off to safety through their grass:

There they re-grouped to watch us. For they were
Neither wild nor tame, the quiet man said
Lighting the candles at the strange hotel
Talking softly with the hidden girl
Behind the kitchen door; padding to table,
Sweeping plates up with an airy hand.
Already it seemed strange that he should do this
Being white. His Siamese kitten ran
With fluffed, and smoky ears, beneath our feet.

The kitten could be scooped up. But the oryx –
Today I trudge a mile along the road
In crushed white dust: more brilliant than my skirts.
Once these deer were bottle-fed, they stayed
Outside the kitchen, at his brother's farm – I walk,
The white stone creeps inside my shoes,
A woman in a blue truck sweeps to halt,
Shouts: 'Do you want a lift?' Is she his mother?
She drives on, wrapped in dust, when I refuse.

Look through the light to the acacia tree.
The wind dies out in heat; the green roof spreads.
Something stands below: too still for grass,
When I shift, it moves, but airily,
Half-afraid. Is neither wild nor tame.
I stand, in my rash scarlet coat, to wait.

We wait together – Soon the sky-blue truck
Whirling in its dust, must re-appear.
Light as I move it moves, in slow, brown dance,
Lover and hunter, who will not come near.

Hippo Pool

Where is the pool? A bicycle gleams –
upside-down – by a hump of rock
whose boiling bubbles broke, and froze.
A man walks slowly out of shade
in a ranger's cream uniform. But, he is black –

I have grown used (after fifteen days)
to see nameless black people pad to the table,
wait by fast roads; bend scolded in kitchens,
sweep dust beneath trees into useless swirls.
This man points ahead, with authority.

We clamber his rock 'to the Bushman painting.'
A lizard's blue tail streaks away.
The man jabs his stick through the iron bars.
See? an impala: red and taut,
a white, giraffe ghost. Were they faint gods,
prayers for hunting? Did a hand
reach, to hold them out of night?

From shaking rungs, on the high rock
we shade our eyes. The reeds toss white
round empty water – 'The hippo are gone;
it is too hot; they went down river.'
He shows us, smiling, the swallows' nest.
'The swallows too have gone – to England.'
So what is left? The cliffs' white fig,
whose roots snake down to feed from stone.

'That is the fence. The Park ends there.
The mountain – see? – is Mozambique.'
The slopes are glowing, like blue coals.
I do not praise the crucible.
I am afraid of fire.
Later we see the blue and brown
of smoke above the piled clouds –
Giraffes' heads turn from tearing thorn.
Is it the rangers, burning scrub:
is it the distant war?

At night, we cross a valley where
steelworks glitter with cats' eyes.
Men, without wives or children, live
in cabins, windowed with neat blinds.
But all across the valley hangs
a yellow smoke, to pierce each crack
reach throats and sting our eyes, as foul
as breath of a great beast: dying.

The hippos have gone
to the kingfisher's pool
where green melts blue, the terrapin
clambers on stone to drown in sun.
Where violet lilies glow, and rise,
the kingfisher waits on a dried twig
hunched, intent. I cannot say
if he is blue as the cloudless sky,
white, as the sea of eyes.

I have not gone there, nor have you,
nor anybody: white or black,
honey-skinned. I only see
tall shapes cross roads, before the night.
Smoke-swift that river runs,
they form against the dust's dead light,
their children's children's sons.

Christmas Roses

December. By now, the catalogues will have been sent:
the seeds, the huge Dutch bulbs, and – all that mattered – the
    roses.
Remember them in our offices, spilling off chairs?
on the cover, some lemon-tipped miniature,
or, in a bad year, the latest Mauve Wonder?
Whoever wanted a purple rose? Anyone – sitting in slippers,
or in scuffed boots, gulping dark tea or gold whisky,
who turns, at last, to their catalogue; sees there, my asterisked
    name.

For I am on every list. I bred one rose,
with finest tints of apple-flower. I died two years ago.

When I was young there were orchards everywhere: tended.
Then cows were turned in them, square and silk,
snuffling the grey bark, hobbling the dusk.
Then the builders came; who could always plead
the need for more houses. I did not see need
to build in so many orchards.

The rose I grew – page twenty-three –
has crinkled flowers: white veined with red,
in broken lines so fine you'd think
it smudged with pink. Man, use your eyes!

Each year the wind swept off the fen
we set more panes in the great house
which kept my new stock from the frost.
Only Mauve Wonders, then the crafty
packing charges, met our loss.

Now, if my son has let it stand
eyeless to the blackest gales
I do not care – I might be glad.

For in the first year, fresh to death,
I thought: if I had time again
I would have bred a sterner rose,
its white as bare as cloud, or frost,
(but not as smiles that watch the dead).
Or I would grow it scarlet, deep –
never so warm – as hearts' quick blood.

The disillusioned men, who bred
the first tamed roses, willed them hard
as their war colours; crimson throbbed
their chosen petals; purple jarred
against the whiteness of their stock.

As I grew out in my next year,
I passed, with winds, across the world.
All I had done, all, once, I loved,
entrusted to the clear walls, whirled
away from me. My roses fed
no living mouth. I stole my bread.

What shall I find in my third year?
The tea-steam blooms along the panes
while tired eyes lose their place, the light's flower closes.
Living, dead, we stay at war. The scratches,
black in the glass, were not the work of roses.